A GUIDE TO

THE ART OF BEING HUMAN

Third Edition

Joan McElligott Cronin, ed.

Miami-Dade Community College

HARPER & ROW, PUBLISHERS, New York
Cambridge, Philadelphia, San Francisco, London,
Mexico City, São Paulo, Singapore, Sydney

A Guide to The Art of Being Human, Third Edition

Copyright © 1988 by Miami-Dade Community College

ISBN: 0-06-043253-5

89 90 91 92 93 9 8 7 6 5 4 3 2 1

CONTENTS

		Page
Preface		v
General Goals of the Course		vii
General Learning Objectives		ix
On Using This Study Guide		xi

MODULE

I	Being Human	1
II	Art and the Artists	15
	Survey 1	22
III	Music: The Planned Environment	29
IV	Drama and Film	37
	Survey 2	54
V	Philosophy: The Question of Reality	63
VI	Philosophy: Moral Values	79
	Survey 3	87
VII	Drama: Eastern/Western Consciousness	95
VIII	Critical Thinking	107
	Survey 4	117
IX	Themes in the Humanities: Myth	125
X	Themes in the Humanities: Love	141
	Survey 5	148
XI	Themes in the Humanities: Happiness	155
XII	Themes in the Humanities: Coping with Death	163
	Survey 6	171
XIII	Themes in the Humanities: Apollo and Dionysus	179
XIV	Themes in the Humanities: The Mechanical Mystique	187
	Survey 7	195
XV	Themes in the Humanities: Freedom	203
	Survey 8	212

A PREFACE TO THIS COURSE

Since the title of this course is <u>The Art of Being Human</u>, one can rightly assume that it rests upon a crucial distinction between the human qualities which belong to everyone (such as the need to survive, to find adequate food and shelter, to reproduce, and so on) and those human qualities about which we have some choice. These are the life-enhancing qualities: the love of the beautiful, the need to think, the desire to associate with others who want to do more with their lives than is absolutely essential to "getting along."

In this course one who seeks to cultivate the art of living is called a humanist. It is taken for granted that this art can take many forms and can be known through many different styles. It is taken for granted that the capacity to practice the art is not limited to an elite group of well-educated persons but exists as a potential in all human beings. But, unfortunately, the practice takes time and effort. Many prefer not to make the investment.

The art of living includes thinking about matters not directly related to the needs of the moment--matters such as whether there is a God and whether love is more than a myth created by the poets. It also involves keeping in touch with one's feelings. (Am I happy? Am I afraid to die?) It is being sensitive and alive to both the physical and the social environment, not to mention spending time in the company of the philosophers, the poets and artists, the composers and dramatists. And it is more that will be made clear as the course unfolds.

In this course humanism, which is the approach to life of the person dedicated to realizing his human potential, is not tied in with material goals. These may at times be rightly prized, but the self-realized person recognizes that money, possessions, power, and status are not the things that make living burst into song or tremble with excitement.

Perhaps the months spent in the company of artists and songsters, of mythmakers and players, of crashing waves and solitary birds...will in the long run lead to a reevaluation of how one stands with respect to the material goals, with respect to many things, in fact, including one's sense of total well-being in this world as a person. Eventually one may make decisions about one's path of life that would have been unimaginable two years ago--or a month ago.

Anyway, we have designed this course believing that many things are worth indulging in for their own sake, and not for the sake of "just" surviving or of upgrading one's position in this world. Humanism may involve everything that is left over after we have done the obvious things and still wonder whether there might not be something missing.

THE ART OF BEING HUMAN Course Team

Marjorie Buhr   Betsy Hilbert
Joan Cronin   Richard Janaro
Donald Early   Richard Price
Ruth Greenfield

GENERAL GOALS OF THE COURSE

1. To recognize that the art of being human involves more than meeting one's survival needs, physiological and psychological.

2. To recognize one's inner resources for practicing the art of being human.

3. To identify a reasonable number of the great philosophical ideas.

4. To recognize philosophical ideas which have personal significance.

5. To recognize religious and non-religious foundations for moral values.

6. To become familiar with characteristics of recognized works of art, music, literature and drama that are encountered during the course.

7. To be willing to listen to and discuss points of view that are different from one's own.

8. To develop an interest in local resources in the arts.

9. To evaluate works of art, music, or drama, utilizing the fundamentals of critical analysis.

10. To develop techniques for critical thinking.

GENERAL LEARNING OBJECTIVES

The learning objectives for each module appear in the individual chapters, but the following is a list of the general objectives which will be satisfied by the time the course is ended.

1. The student will demonstrate a knowledge of terminology from each of the humanities areas by recalling and defining selected terms which are essential for understanding the subject matter.
   (Satisfied by all modules.)

2. The student will demonstrate a knowledge of the humanities by identifying perspectives, views, and content of the humanities.
   (Satisfied by all modules, but especially by Module I.)

3. The student will demonstrate a knowledge of the humanities by relating chosen major works to their creators, eras, and cultures.
   (Satisfied by Modules II, III, XIII, and XV.)

4. The student will demonstrate a knowledge of philosophers and their thinking by recognizing the tenets of their theories.
   (Satisfied by Modules V, VI, VII X, XII, and XV.

5. The student will demonstrate some familiarity with forms, media, and stypes of art, architecture, music, literature, and drama by explaining specific works in each of the above areas.
   (Satisfied by the following modules:
   Art, Module II
   Architecture, Module II
   Drama, Module IV
   Literature, Modules I. IV, IX, X, XI, XII, XIII
   Music, Module III.)

6. The student will demonstrate analysis of arts and philosophies of various Western and non-Western cultures by comparing major creative contributions.
   (Satisfied by Module VI.)

7. The student will demonstrate analysis of the relationship among the humanities by interrelating philosophic and artistic developments of various historical periods.
   (Satisfied by Modules IV, V, XI, XIII, and XV.)

8. The student will demonstrate comprehension of facts and concepts pertaining to the humanities by paraphrasing them.
   (Satisfied by essay options on examinations.)

9. The student will demonstrate analysis of selected examples of works in the humanities by comparing forms, media, styles, and philosophies.
   (Satisfied by selecting appropriate Bonus Point options.)

10. The student will demonstrate a regard for the value of the humanities by discussing its personal impact.
    (Satisfied by essay options on examinations.)

The following six objectives can be met by those students who elect to submit Bonus Point Essays.

1. The student will demonstrate willingness to respond to the roles the humanities play in community life by selecting and reporting on events and works of art found in the community or on the college campus that are related to course discussion and reading.

2. The student will demonstrate evaluation by developing and applying criteria of judgment to selected works from each of the humanities.

3. The student will demonstrate a willingness to respond to the uniqueness of the creative process by sharing with others an appreciation of creative methods used in various media.

4. The student will demonstrate a willingness to respond to multicultural diversity and accomplishment by discussing these achievements and their impact on society.

5. The student will demonstrate a willingness to evaluate achievements in the humanities by substantiating his/her value judgments.

6. The student will demonstrate a synthesis of ideas acquired through studying humanities by organizing and communicating those ideas effectively in writing.

ON USING THIS STUDY GUIDE

The Study Guide has four main functions: 1) to tie together the video and text components of the course and to point out common themes and concerns; 2) to help you focus the major ideas in each module; 3) to provide sample test questions on several levels of difficulty; and 4) to suggest how to structure your participation in the course.

Each module begins with an Overview, which you should study carefully before reading the text chapter or viewing the TV programs. The learning objectives for the module come next, and we advise you to familiarize yourself with these in the beginning and then to look long and hard at them before answering the Survey questions or preparing to take the course examinations.

Assistance in reading and viewing follows the learning objectives, and, while you may elect to watch the TV programs before reading the text or Study Guide, we highly recommend that you come to the programs with an understanding of the basic subject matter of the module.

The TV programs are <u>not</u> restatements of the material which appears in the text. Nor are they televised lectures on each subject. They are, rather, independent works--in some cases actual dramas--relevant to the issues at hand, but often aiming at an emotional impact. If you have some grasp of the issues you will be able to sit back and enjoy each program without being distracted by the need to take notes or to work out its meaning <u>during</u> the viewing.

Each module in the Study Guide contains a Self-Test, consisting of matching items, relating to both the text and the programs. This test has both obvious and obscure items; it is intended to provoke you to review critically important concepts. We urge you to review carefully the Check List of Main Ideas and to make sure you understand them.

Each Survey contains a minimum of 20 multiple choice questions taken from the two preceding modules, except for Survey 8, which relates only to Module XV. These are sample questions and suggest not only the kind of material that will be useful to know, but the various <u>levels</u> on which questions can be written. Some questions merely ask for opinions and therefore have no right or wrong answers. The Study Guide does not offer correct or possible responses to the Survey items. These will be provided by the instructor.

One last suggestion: By now the course has been running for several years. Statistics convincingly indicate that the most successful students are those who do the Surveys, receive feedback, and review the material with others.

MODULE I

Being Human

OVERVIEW

The title of this course is intended to raise some questions about what it means to be human rather than to make a definitive statement. Of course "human" has definite biological connotations, and simply by being born most persons achieve in a biological sense the "essence of being human."

On the other hand, connotations other than the biological exist, and thus it is in another sense that this course recognizes "human" to refer to what could be called the "developed" faculties: intellect, rationality, and sensitivity to form.

Being human can be a random, accidental, "come-what-may" existence or a deliberate actualization of one's full potential. The course takes the view that one can deliberately make more of one's humanness.

The humanities are the disciplines that provide people with resources for engaging in humanistic concerns and leading a satisfying existence. They include the arts, religion, philosophy, architecture, history, and those aspects of social and physical sciences which affect the quality and conduct of human life.

People who make the most of their humanness are the ones who make time in their everyday lives to read, to think, to experience new ways of seeing, more complete ways of being. They sing, dance, paint. They frequent theaters, art galleries, concert halls. They notice and respect their environment. They also concern themselves with the quality of other lives.

Foremost among the more evident features of their way of life is the recognition that people have a choice. People may leave their lives alone, making little or no effort to sharpen their higher faculties. Or they can decide that there are so many thoughts to think, so many emotions to feel, so many musical notes to hear that one lifetime cannot possibly be long enough. It is very hard for them to be bored.

Woodrow Tatlock, in The Man with No Time for Beauty, would be a good example of a person who has not made the effort to sharpen his higher faculties. He has been totally unchanged by experience. He has settled for too little.

Living the fully actualized life can be a very lonely path, for society often settles for the very least, not the very best, of which one is capable. Those who choose to think and to question, those who read avidly, those who continue to wonder why--run the risk of being stared at, or worse. They may, indeed, seem as eccentric as the mimes in The Way of the Humanist. But, as you will note, the mimes go their placid way, untroubled--although there may be significance in the fact that they are not heard.

1

LEARNING OBJECTIVES

Having completed this module, you should be able to

1) recognize characteristics of those who go through life with or without a background in the humanities, as presented in the text and TV programs.

2) explain in your own words what form means in areas of human life such as sports, social affairs, business.

3) recognize the importance of form in works of art.

AS YOU READ

Introduction: "To Be Human"

1. Your text declines to be a history of Western culture. Summarize the reasons for this position.

2. In your own words, can you indicate why the character of Woodrow is introduced in this first chapter? Describe Woodrow. Are there many people like him? Suppose he were to object, as well he might, "I like my life just the way it is." Can you offer him a meaningful alternative to that life?

3. Distinguish between the several uses of the word "living" as they appear in the chapter.

4. The chapter argues that the past has its right to exist. Why? What can be said about a person who denies that right, who has no interest in learning anything about the past? Can't one lead a satisfying life without such knowledge?

5. Summarize the characteristics of the fully realized human being as these are set forth in the chapter. (It would be a good idea to keep these in mind as you go through the course.)

6. Define the term _form_ as it is to be used throughout this text.

7. The need for completeness appears to be a uniquely human phenomenon. Show the relationship between this need and the desire for form.

8. Explain the relationship between forms and cultures.

VIEWING

I.   The Man with No Time for Beauty

    --The actor who played Woodrow Tatlock did not actually accompany the students
      to Europe to make this film. Look for ways in which the illusion is created
      that he was really there.

    --"Assuming the sense of the beautiful to have been implicit from very early
      times, why is it that so many (like Woodrow Tatlock) appear to get along without
      heeding it?" Certain conditions isolate individuals from a perception of the
      beautiful: the closed-mind, the self-satisfied attitude, the false conception,
      the banal cliché about art, and many others. Woodrow takes all of these as
      mental baggage on his European tour and, alas, brings them back with him
      virtually intact.

    --"The difference between the child and the adult is that the adult sees what
      is himself and the child is what he sees." This statement is reinforced
      visually in the close-up details of Woodrow's living room, containing his own
      "personal culture." One of the terrible things that can happen to us as we grow
      older is to lose the capacity to experience what is to be experienced; we become
      highly selective, responding only to those stimuli which immediately concern us
      or reinforce our opinions. Thus, the person who thinks all operas are full of
      fat people making funny sounds with their voices, will listen to no opera at
      all.

    --The difference between the imaginative child and the less imaginative adult
      is a major theme not only in this program but throughout the entire course.
      Inevitably, much that belongs to childhood must be lost as we grow up (Woodrow
      once drew birds and a picture of morning with colored crayons). But, thank-
      fully, not all of it. We are still able to respond with delight to uninhibited
      children's art--to recognize its freshness, its unqualified truth, its direct
      experience of the child's world. Artists, perhaps, retain more of this child-
      like clarity of perception than the rest of us. Indeed, it is the lack of this
      quality that makes many of us dismiss much that is fine in modern art as
      "childish"--works by Picasso, Matisse, Klee, Miro, and others. We must look to
      the artist to preserve a home for the child we once were, where we can again
      look out on the world with wide, unclouded eyes.

    --"Does the past matter?" We hear this question asked with growing frequency
      today--especially by the young--as if only the living present existed, and never
      the living past. Yet a culture carries its past with it, alive and generative,
      just the way an individual does. We can understand about people who suffer
      amnesia and who forget their past, that is, their sense of self-continuity, of
      continuous identity. But we may not understand that this can happen to a
      society as well. No society can be sound and able to perpetuate itself if
      contact with its roots, its sources of identity, is lost. The great art of the
      past--always as much a group expression as the product of the artist's mind--is
      the substance of our cultural identity, the touchstone that tells us what we are
      in time and place and spirit. In this unit, Woodrow Tatlock's introduction to
      some portions of the past, though it leaves him untouched, serves to put us in
      touch with a part of ourselves we may have mislaid or never really understood.

3

--As you look at the program, pay some attention to the different architectural landmarks that Woodrow and the student visit.

The Louvre, the national art museum of France, is an example of Baroque architecture, which flourished in the seventeenth and eighteenth centuries. Baroque architecture was based on the classical orders but interpreted them quite freely, making use of curves and flowing forms, dramatic contrasts in light and shade, sensuous color, and a sense of overall unity emerging from varied, complex elements.

The Louvre was begun as a royal residence by Francis I in 1546, and underwent many architectural changes before its completion in the nineteenth century. The more recent east facade, for instance, does not look at all Baroque (in contrast with the building on the Ringstrasse in Vienna); however, other features such as the complex, curved vaulting, place the Louvre within the Baroque tradition.

The Royal Palace of Madrid, begun by Philip V in 1737, is another example of Baroque architecture. The massive, twisted pillars give a sense of energy and grandeur that characterize the Baroque. Typically Baroque, too, is the play of light and shadow given by the entablature and projecting wings.

The Cathedral of Milan is an example of late Gothic architecture. The term Gothic was originally a reference to the culture of the Goths, a warlike Germanic tribe that overran the Roman Empire early in the fifth century A.D. During the post-Roman period, which ushered in the medieval world, the Christian Church spread throughout Europe, creating a new style of civilization. The term Gothic gradually became a designation for the art and architecture of the later Middle Ages. The Gothic cathedral, perhaps the outstanding single example of this movement, is characterized by pointed arches, flying buttresses, rib vaults, pinnacles, and stained glass windows.

In contrast to the sense of unity achieved in Baroque architecture, an impression of infinite complexity emerges from the details of the Gothic cathedral. And in contrast to the dramatic light and shadow in Baroque buildings, an evenly diffused and rather unearthly light pervades the Gothic interior through stained glass windows.

The viewer can see an example of supreme achievement in stained glass in The Way of the Humanist. The rose window of Sainte Chapelle in Paris appears as the narrator is saying, "I saw . . . that the real strength of human beings was their determination to go ahead anyway. . . to put their mark upon the earth . . ."

Experts argued from 1386 to 1401 over a design that would ensure the stability of the vast structure planned for the Milan Cathedral. The result of the long debate was a compromise: rather broad in relation to its height, the Cathedral differs from traditionally tall, slender Gothic buildings, but it is typically Gothic in its profusion of pinnacles, balustrades, and elaborate tracery.

4

The <u>Galleria</u> in Milan is surely one of the older shopping malls in the world. An architectural feature of note is the elaborate floor design, which is built in the shape of a cross, resembling the floor plan of a cathedral. This resemblance is further supported by an enormous glass dome which covers the central area of the mall.

The <u>Schönbrunn</u> (name means "beautiful fountain") is a Baroque palace outside Vienna, a city that is itself a treasure trove of Baroque buildings. In 1694 Emperor Leopold I conceived the idea of building at Schönbrunn an imperial residence to outshine that of his rival, Louis XIV, at Versailles. In the Baroque tradition, the gardens complement the design of the building.

The <u>Hermitage</u> in Leningrad is the largest public museum and art gallery in Russia. The art collection that would be stored in the Heritage was begun by Peter the Great and continued by Catherine the Great--one of the most avid art collectors of all time. Although you see only the interior of the Hermitage, standing outside you would be able to observe the bulbous or onion-shaped domes crowning the building. These domes, characteristic of Russian architecture, can be seen in the panorama of Leningrad when Woodrow and his party first arrive.

II. <u>The Way of the Humanist</u>

--The little girl with her vague, unfulfilled longings for "something more" than she finds in the schoolroom suggests that we are not born with the knowledge of how to live a fully human life, though we have certain resources that, unfortunately, are often allowed to remain dormant. One of these is imagination. Note that poetry is the girl's favorite subject.

--The motif of childhood imagination runs throughout the course. Picasso once wrote: "Every child is an artist. The problem is how to remain an artist once he grows up." These wonderful lines sum up a major thesis of this course.

--The poem experienced by the girl in the opening sequence is the sonnet "After Dark Vapours Have Oppress'd Our Plains" by John Keats (1791-1821). While the child responds mainly to the sensuous beauty of Keats's words and images, the viewer needs to be aware that Keats, who died at twenty-five, was preoccupied with thoughts of death. In fact, the final and most beautiful idea that comes to him in association with this first true day of spring is of his own death. The poem therefore is meant to suggest that the viewer can find wonder and joy in this world while also accepting its sorrow.

--The young lady mime travels abroad, first visiting Italy, which gave birth to the Renaissance during the 14th century. The term Renaissance means "rebirth," referring to such things as innovations in art and architecture, the development of the modern idea of the city, the questioning of the medieval Church's absolute authority, and a newfound faith in the unlimited potential of mankind. During the Middle Ages, Christianity looked upon humanity as being the eternal child of God the Father, forever bounded by an imperfect intellect and moral nature. The Renaissance rejected the notion of boundaries, introducing a new form of humanism, one that said people could achieve the perfection once attributed solely to God. The Renaissance world was dominated by individual greatness, but the important point made by the narrator is that "they were people just like me." In other words, in this course "Renaissance" is more than a historical movement; it is the ever-existing possibility of personal growth.

--Leonardo da Vinci has particular significance for the narrator, for here was indeed the ideal of the Renaissance--the fully actualized human being. Not only did his genius express itself in painting, sculpture, and architecture, but he was also a biologist, a military strategist, and an inventor whose achievements ran far ahead of many developments in modern technology (e.g., the airplane and the submarine).

--The name "Buddha" signifies "the awakened one." In Buddhist thought, to be awake is to be totally aware of the world around and within us. It is to participate with our total being--mind, body, and senses--in everything that exists. Observe that this view of life is shared to some extent by the writers and artists represented in this film.

--The narrator suggests that for the Buddhist the unity of all being represents "love in a wonderful kind of way, because it is never lost." In this context "love" is not used romantically, but rather as a poetic expression of that unity, the oneness of all living beings through the fact that existence is always equal to itself no matter how many different forms it takes.

--As the mime lies dying, his soul quotes Walter Pater's famous lines from The Renaissance: "Every moment some form grows perfect in hand or face; some tone on the hills or sea is choicer than the rest..." In this work Pater wrote that, because life passes so quickly, it is our human obligation to enjoy each day, to relish all sensations, all passions.

--After the death of the male mime, the female mime is seen walking along a riverbank. The narrator quotes lines from Tennyson's poem In Memoriam, written on the death of a beloved fried of the poet. In it Tennyson expresses doubts about the meaning of life and man's purpose in the world; but the poet finally comes to accept his loss and to voice his faith that people achieve immortality through what they leave behind. The lines quoted suggest to the viewer that, while a humanist may die, humanism will not.

--You will notice that in the first poster the mime is wearing a top hat and carrying a cane; but in the last poster these are missing. Think about the symbolism, as the girl now holds the hat and cane. Ask yourself, also, why the central character is shown once again as a child.

SELF-TEST

Now that you have read the text and Study Guide Chapters and have viewed the two programs which accompany Module I, you may wish to determine how much you have learned. Matching tests conclude this and all other modules of the course. No item in the second column may be used more than once, so, in some instances, you will be faced with making the best, not necessarily the only choice.

The degree of difficulty in these self-tests is fairly high: that is , they are comprehensive. You have the advantage of looking back over the print materials and refreshing your memory of the video programs (items marked T are taken from the textbook; those marked V are from the video programs). The theory is that, if you can match the items accurately, you stand a good change of being able to handle examination questions without much trouble. Answers can be found at the back of this Study Guide.

V 1.	Leonardo da Vinci	spending public money for art	8
V 2.	Santa Maria del Fiore	the rightness of an arrangement	10
VT 3.	Moby Dick	genius in both art and science	2
V 4.	The Great Maestoso	reverses stereotyped roles	4
V 5.	Michelangelo	creativity and imagination	1 9
V 6.	Woodrow as a child	esthetic pleasure in repetition of forms	12
T 7.	form	completeness for its own sake	7
V 8.	Woodrow disapproved of it	strange to Western playgoers	11
V 9.	the silent movie	left his hat behind	
T 10.	tea ceremony	believed a failure in its own time	3
T 11.	Kabuki	wouldn't compromise on a painting	5
T 12	folk song	example of the living past	6

7

CHECK LIST OF MAIN IDEAS

1. A study of the humanities should encompass more than the life and work of a relatively few artists and philosophers; it should offer a whole approach to living--acessible to all people--in which one makes full use of creative and intellectual resources in order to enhance the quality of one's life.

2. A good reason that some people have no time for beauty, making contact with the past and empathizing with other people, is their inability to consider anything more important than themselves.

3. Being human may be inborn, but the art of being human is not. It has to be acquired. No one can, however, force you to acquire it. You alone must initiate the drive.

4. One term that links all the humanities and seems to distinguish humankind from the other species is form. Human beings seek and create form in all their activities--social, professional, esthetic, and even recreational.

ON THE REALITY OF THE BEAUTIFUL

by

Donald M. Early

Humankind, says contemporary depth psychology, has an innate capacity to apprehend the beautiful. But what does this mean? To apprehend means "to become aware of, to perceive; to recognize the meaning of . . ." A capacity that is innate must be one that is universal, present everywhere, in every culture. And anthropology does indeed confirm that no human group exists that does not have some form of art--does not both "apprehend the beautiful" and practice it too, by creating some form of beauty of its own.

How shall we explain this phenomenon? Shall we look to psychology for the answer, since it tells us so much about the hidden processes of our minds? No, for both Freud and Jung declare that "psychoanalysis has nothing to say about aesthetics," and that "the problem can never be the object of psychological, but only of an aesthetic-artistic method of approach." It would appear then that the answer lies much deeper, in more ancient soil--in our biology, in the very nature and structure of the world itself.

No one will deny that the world is beautiful. Daily and nightly, season by season, creation unfolds its inexhaustible splendors. And we in our humdrum lives, while not unmindful of its beauty, tend to notice it only at favored moments, when we experience beauty as an event: a sunset, a snowfall, the sound of wind and water, the sight and perfume of an orchard in bloom. Yet, the pageant of beauty never pauses, never diminishes, even when we do not attend it. "The Rainbow comes and goes/And lovely is the Rose," the poet would have us remember.

The crucial question seems to be this: is beauty in the thing we behold, or is it in the eye of the beholder? "Is the birdsong in the tree, or in me?" we ask. The philosopher in us may find the question intriguing (remember the old classroom puzzle: if a tree falls in the forest and no one is there to hear it, is there a sound?); but the poet in us may already know the answer.

Surely the world was beautiful long before human eyes were there to witness it. Picture how many eons Earth must have spun in its azure envelope of light in space before the moonshot showed us its breathtaking splendor. Then consider the case of flowers. Loren Eisley, in his book The Immense Journey, tells us that the flowering world as we know it came into being at the same time as the first mammals. Suddenly, it seems, in what can only be described as a veritable explosion of life, incredible numbers of flowering plants appeared, filling the atmosphere with their perfumes, blooming with a prodigality that cannot possibly be accounted for in terms of survival value alone. Such exuberance, proliferating in an infinite variety of beautiful forms and colors, was far in excess of nature's extravagant requirements for preservation. Was this simultaneous advent of flowers and mammals purely coincidental--or were the two related? Can it be that nature, having produced creatures of a higher order capable of perceiving the results, was then inspired to a frenzy of artistic creation--for the sheer joy of virtuosity, for the sheer beauty of it?

Is there, one wonders, a principle in nature that eludes us? Can beauty be a force, a law, a condition of the created world--like gravitation? The scientist may shy away from the idea, but the aesthetician, who studies the nature of the beautiful, and the artist who strives to create the beautiful, will not. Both are convinced that they work according to certain laws of nature, of reality, of their own being; both believe that they are as much in pursuit of Truth as the scientist.

The problem leads back to ourselves, of course. We are creatures of the universe, and whatever universal laws exist must be as evident in us as anywhere else in the cosmos. What then are the laws that guide us in our apprehension of beauty, in the creation of beautiful forms, colors, sounds, odors, sensations?

One of these is the law of sexuality. Beauty attracts, draws us toward a union with itself, whether it be beauty of body, mind, or spirit. In the presence of beauty we are as lovers; and we may find ourselves as dazzled, as swept with delight or terror, as if we were in the throes of a powerful passion. The element of sexuality can never be wholly absent from any experience of beauty. What Nietzsche sagely remarked of the individual can be said as well of the race: "The degree and kind of a person's sexuality reaches up into the ultimate pinnacle of his spirit." This must not be taken to mean that a work of divine aspiration, such as Chartres Cathedral, has overt erotic intent; nothing would be more absurd. Yet the purpose of this great work of art is to lead the worshiper through avenues of beauty--some of the sense, others of the spirit--to an eventual union with God.

Nature's laws, says the noted art critic Herbert Read, are the touchstone for all human creativity, though he warns: "We must understand by nature not any vague pantheistic spirit, but the measurements and physical behavior of matter in any process of growth or transformation. The seed that becomes a flowering plant, the metal that crystallizes as it cools and contracts, all such processes exhibit laws, which are modes of material behavior. There is no growth which is not accompanied by its characteristic form, and I think we are so constituted--are so much in sympathy with natural processes--that we always find such form beautiful."

When man creates a work of beauty, he does so intuitively, according to these laws. The "rules" of a work of art are the proportions and rhythms inherent in the universe. The artist perceives these, usually more clearly than the rest of us, though his perceptions may not always be conscious ones. "Artists," explains Read, "are to a considerable degree automata...that is, they unwittingly transmit in their works a sense of scale, proportion, symmetry, balance, and other abstract qualities which they have acquired through their purely visual and therefore physical response to the natural environment."

Another critic puts it this way: "Things take on the life of their creators, but their spirit derives from a common source which goes back to the origins of the universe, of mankind, of our respective civilizations, back to our birth and are constantly revitalized with the dawn of each new day."

Too many of us have minds so clogged with the impediments of a banal culture, our vision so clouded with falsely ordered impressions, that we have lost the habit of responding spontaneously to aesthetic experience. We have grown dull to what Bernard Berenson calls "the aesthetic moment, that flitting instant, so brief as to be almost timeless, when the spectator...ceases to be his ordinary self, and the picture or building, statue, landscape, or aesthetic actuality is no longer outside himself...The two become one entity; time and space are abolished and the spectator is possessed by one awareness." Our lack of awareness of the aesthetic moment is in part the result of our technological culture, our scientific approach to the world. We are conditioned to think analytically, to look for the elements of a thing and not at the thing itself. The psychologist will tell us that we have emphasized the function of the left (analytical) lobe of the brain to the neglect of that of the right lobe, which perceives things whole. Whatever the cause, true esthetic experience can come about only when our responses are not impeded by "thinking too precisely upon the point." Beauty asks for a spontaneous union; and when too many clauses and conditions invest the contract, the marriage does not take place.

Spontaneity, however, in no way precludes a knowledge of those natural laws that inform the esthetic moment. Paleolithic man was not without a canon of esthetics; he already had a highly sophisticated understanding of his art. Indeed, the renowned paleontologist Abbe Breuil speculates that "there were colleges of artists, far from each other, but subject to the conventions and same fashions... institutions which directed and...created uniformity of expressions." Remains of sketch books--bone fragments covered with thousands of beginners' "life studies"--have been found which lend support to this scholar's assumption.

So the call is not to "return to the primitive" in order to clarify our vision and see things fresh. Quite the reverse. "It takes a mature mind and a great deal of living," says Bruno Bettelheim "to bear in oneself a vision of the better world for which the real artist (paleolithic or modern) is striving and then embodies in aesthetic form." Growth's direction is always forward, not backward. But growth demands effort; and the man who would have time for beauty must make the effort to get in touch with himself.

A noted architect who designs structures of extraordinary "rightness" has this to say of his own self-awareness: "The pleasurable intensity of my responses to certain buildings, seen for the first time, suggests to me that they must somehow correspond to a model which already exists deep inside me. How else can I account for the sensation so much closer to recognition than to discovery? This, I believe, is the revelation of the self to the self."

The artist who sees more "rightly" than the rest of us helps us to remedy our defective vision, to sharpen our aesthetic sensibilities, to respond more intuitively and truthfully to the world of beauty around us. Who, one wonders, every saw--really saw--a sunflower, until van Gogh showed us what a sunflower looks like?

We learn, we grow, we increase in awareness and spirit to the degree that we harmonize with nature--all nature--our own most of all. Too many of us lead lives that are discordant, having no real time for beauty...

11

The story is told of a man who died and came before God. And the Creator of the Universe, looking down, inquired, "Well, what did you think of my little world?" The man was silent. "Didn't you find it beautiful?" urged the Questioner. Finally, ashamed to raise his head, the man replied, "I didn't really notice, Lord... I never seemed to have the time..."

How very sad.

RECOMMENDED READING*

Alan Bloom. <u>The Closing of the American Mind</u> (New York: Simon and Schuster, 1987). The thesis is that because education has become more permissive in recent decades, standards by which we learn to evaluate the world around us have become so relative as to be meaningless. Only that which has immediate relevance has value. Yet, he insists, the past deserves to be preserved.

Elaine Cannel. <u>Good Taste: How to Have It, How to Buy It</u> (New York: David McKay, 1978). The premise of this book is that good taste exists as an objective faculty which some people have, others can acquire, and everybody needs if we are to live in a truly civilized way.

Kenneth Clark. <u>Civilisation: A Personal View</u> (New York: Harper & Row, 1970). An excellent historical overview of the humanities, recommended for those who would like a chronological frame of reference.

Gillo Dorfles. Kitsch: <u>The World of Bad Taste</u> (New York: Bell, 1968). This funny book can infuriate you if you happen to find some of your own prized possessions among those illustrated. As the author points out, "one man's kitsch is another man's living room." The illustrations include many advertisements which exploit our apparently easy susceptibility to cheap sentiment, the essence of kitsch.

Abraham Maslow. <u>Toward a Psychology of Being</u> (Princeton, N.J.: Van Nostrand, 1962). This major work by one of the founders of the movement known as humanistic psychology provides an excellent foundation for comprehending the new humanism, which fundamentally states that meeting basic needs is not enough for a fulfilled life.

Thorstein Veblen. <u>The Theory of the Leisure Class</u> (New York, Modern Library, 1934). This study of the value system and the taste of America's moneyed elite was originally published in 1899, but the author's insights may strike you as quite contemporary.

*Some of the Recommend Readings reinforce the views presented in this course. Some may challenge it. Some may offer interesting, if highly controversial, alternatives. In drawing up the brief but select lists of readings, the authors have been guided by the desire to stimulate and to provoke thought on the reader's part.

MODULE II

Art and the Artist

OVERVIEW

From Stone Age cave paintings, in which early man attempted to gain control over his quarry by capturing their images, to contemporary abstractions, humanity has used art to create its own environment and to achieve a measure of immortality.

The way of the artist, as this module demonstrates, is not always the easiest path on which to travel. While we might blink our eyes at some of the more extreme innovations of today's artists, often wondering by what right some of their works "deserve" to be labeled art, we need to remind ourselves that there has always been modern art, even in the Middle Ages. There are always those in any period who run the risk of public scorn and loss of favor by expressing what they truly feel and in the way they know it should look. In this sense, artists themselves are models of the humanists' decision not to compromise when such a step would inhibit their creativity.

Thus in this module we define art not by the characteristics of a particular age or style, but in terms of the enduring human need to do certain things: stand tall, reach out, alter the environment, imitate nature, and sometimes to create in terms of color, line, and shape what has never existed before.

You are invited to come to art, not with rigid expectations of what it should be, but with an openness that can only result in your own enrichment. If a sculpture that looks like a giant ice bag finally leaves you unmoved, let your evaluation reflect a willingness to give the artist a fair amount of attention.

LEARNING OBJECTIVES

Having completed this module, you should be able to

1) explain the function in human society of artists and their art.

2) cite major examples of both traditional and contemporary approaches to painting and sculpture.

3) specify comparable and contrasting motives in artists of the past and the present.

4) explain the resistance of the medium, the need to imitate or alter, and the surrounding culture as factors in the psychology of the artist.

Chapter 1: "The Way of the Artist"

1. We can achieve a responsible overview of what artists are all about by understanding what Aristotle meant by the term "imitation." In art imitation does not refer to an attempt to make a picture or a carving, for example, look just like the original (although some artists do wish to achieve a realistic likeness). Imitation in art is the process by which the artist seeks to recreate the creative process of nature itself.

2. New theories of art insist that a talent for drawing or painting is not limited to a rare few, but belongs to anyone who takes the time to see.

3. During the Renaissance there occurred a breakthrough in the art of imitating the likeness of reality, and that was the development of perspective. Be sure you can explain what perspective is and how it is achieved. Describe Giotto's contributions to this device.

4. Explain chiaroscuro as a further advance in the technique of transferring reality to the canvas. Describe Rembrandt's importance here.

5. Describe Kienholz' Still Live - 1974 as one example of what a modern sculptor is doing. From the chapter draw forth some reasons that can be used to call this work "art."

6. Make sure you can summarize the controversy over Goya's later work.

7. Be able to explain the phrase "resistance of the medium." Use Michelangelo as the artist whose work supremely illustrates its meaning. Apply to Michelangelo the statement "Art is pretending that there is no artist."

8. What was the response of the impressionists to the development of photography? Distinguish between impressionism and post-impressionism, using Monet and Van Gogh as examples of their respective movements.

9. Summarize the point that is made in the chapter about the position taken by the artist in a developing culture as opposed to a long established culture.

10. What is the Marxist view of art and the artist? Do you believe that a government has the right to determine what should and should not be expressed by artists?

11. What was the dispute between Rockefeller and Rivera? Do the Rockefellers of this world have any justifiable rights when it comes to art? Did the Church have any right to condemn Michelangelo's The Last Judgment?

12. Why is Pablo Picasso regarded as the supreme artist of the 20th century? How is he entitled to such an honor when artists of the immediate present are no longer imitating him?

13. In what respect are Georgia O'Keeffe and Piet Mondrian considered to be precursors of the Minimalists?

14. Describe the work of Edwin Hopper and Duane Hanson. Why are they called artists of alienation?

VIEWING

I. Art: Tell Me What I Am

   Art: Tell Us Who We Are

   --The narrator of this program is an artist, not necessarily a great and famous artist, but perhaps just an ordinary human being who wants to leave something of himself behind, and who needs to project himself into space in some form. Note that he keeps insisting "That's me over there." His attitude is the one which the course adopts as being the true artist's spirit. The motivation of the artist is to reach out and put himself where once there was only a blank wall or space.

   --The materials of art are presented in an almost childlike way. Artists doing art and children doing art are significant parallels used in both this program and Chapter 3 of your text. The premise here is that children have spontaneous creative urges that, alas, are all too often snuffed out in the adult world.

   --Had it not been for its art, Mayan civilization (found in Mexico and Guatemala) probably would not have been recognized. You might wish to draw some parallels with your own life. For example, if you were to vanish tomorrow, would there be any silent witnesses to your having existed?

   --Certain colors express certain emotions and states of mind, evoking these within the viewer. The effects of warm colors can range from gaiety to surging anger; cool colors can evoke discomfort and despair.

   --Many artists (and composers) create bizarre, sometimes disturbing, relationships among the elements in their work. When the butter turns green, and when the lovely young dancing lady turns out to have ugly, protruding teeth, we discover a principle of juxtaposition in art: Putting things together that are unexpected, and that normally do not belong together. This is paralleled by the principle of dissonance in music, which puts nonharmonious sounds together. A question often asked is "What makes such relationships artistic?" Is there an answer?

   --The textures and shapes of things have their own special effects. Sharp, jagged edges given an illusion of pain. Note how Picasso used this effect in his painting, Guernica. Rounded, yielding forms elicit an aura of comfort and pleasure. Why?

   --Lines can be powerful artistic devices. Vertical lines are stable, giving an impression of resoluteness, as illustrated in Michelangelo's statue of David. Goya used strong diagonals to depict motion and urgency. Horizontal lines are quiet; the French painter David used them effectively in his painting, The Death of Marat. Curving lines portray excitement and confusion. Why?

--The artists who appear in the program represent some current trends in art. Although each of them is going in a different direction, they share one particular attitude toward art and the artist. Can you identify this attitude?

II. Divine Discontent

--The title comes from Kenneth Graham's novel, The Wind in the Willows: "Spring was moving in the air above and in the earth below and around him, penetrating even his dark and lowly little house with its spirit of divine discontent and longing." The expression is used here as a reference to the creative out-pourings of some "maladjusted" artists and to their driving need to achieve perfection despite physical and emotional troubles.

--The music you hear throughout the film was composed by Ludwig van Beethoven. Beethoven's sense of a divine mission and his isolation, intensified by deaf-ness, give him an affinity with the artists discussed in this film. The first musical theme is from the Piano Concerto #5, the Emperor. The trio heard is Piano Trio #1 in C Minor.

--Sigmund Freud developed the theory that the artist creates in order to release suppressed sexual urges that society does not tolerate. Freud believed that the genius is mentally unstable, ill-adjusted to society and to his inner self.

--The psychologist Carl Jung took exception to many of Freud's theories. He believed, for example, that the artist is not a pathological personality but rather one of the healthiest members of a society because he expresses unconscious psychic experiences universal to human nature.

--Michelangelo Buonarroti fiercely strove for excellence, striving to please God. When Pope Julius ordered Michelangelo to paint the frescos in the Sistine Chapel, the artist was initially angered because he considered himself a sculptor rather than a painter. Although the Pope had asked only for the figures of the twelve apostles, Michelangelo created instead a design of many hundreds of figures embodying the story of Genesis from the Creation to the Flood. The Sistine ceiling is said to be the only work which Michelangelo felt he was able to complete as he had conceived it.

--Goya's deafness was a highly important factor in his "divine discontent," but so was the decadent state of society. Of the three artists, Goya was the most socially responsive in his work.

--Van Gogh's paintings are unmistakably stamped with his unique style. Most of his great works exhibit bold brush strokes, aggressive use of bright colors, and use of uninterrupted flowing energy--all reflective of his inner turmoil from which he descended into madness and suicide. The final Van Gogh painting shown, The Starry Night, is perhaps his most famous work. It combines all the elements of his style.

Match each item in the first column with an item in the second. Use no item more than one time.

T   1.   Lascaux

T   2.   chiaroscuro

VT 3.   Impressionism

V   4.   critical neglect during lifetime

V   5.   believed that impulse to create art is neurotic

VT 6.   art should lead to social change

T   7.   an instinct implanted in childhood, according to Artistotle

V   8.   "Divine Discontent"

T   9.   Goya

V 10.   juxtaposition in art

T 11.   photography

T 12   Guernica

V 13.   loss of hearing did not mean loss of inspiration

V 14.   Mayan civilization

T 15.   Minimalism

V 16.   vertical lines

V 17.   diagonal lines

T 18.   Black American sculptor

Vincent Van Gogh   _____

express stability and order   _____

the question of whether art can have unpleasant subject matter   _____

created change in purpose and nature of art   _____

putting unrelated things together   _____

art is not to be evaluated for emotional elements   _____

interplay of light and shadow   _____

new light on primitive art   _____

express urgency and motion   _____

Sigmund Freud   _____

Claude Monet   _____

Diego Rivera   _____

known only through its art   _____

Edmonia Lewis   _____

driving need to achieve perfection   _____

Ludwig van Beethoven   _____

Cubist painting   _____

mimesis   _____

CHECK LIST OF MAIN IDEAS

1. People have historically projected themselves into their environment through art.

2. The finest artists need not mirror the taste of the era in which they live, as evidenced by the fact that many artists recognized as great today were ignored or even vilified in their day.

3. The appreciation of art affords enormous personal enrichment. You can enhance your appreciative ability by becoming familiar with works of the past and viewing a large amount of contemporary art with a critical yet open mind.

4. Ideally this gained appreciation will be evidenced in your personal surroundings, which, just as a good work of art reflects the artist's unique being, will be a projection of you.

RECOMMENDED READING

Henry Adams. <u>Mont-Saint-Michel and Chartres</u> (Cambridge, Mass.: The Riverside Press, 1933). In this elegantly written "travelogue," Henry Adams takes the reader back to the 12th and 13th centuries to participate in the events surrounding the construction and life of these French architectural wonders.

Michelangelo Buonarroti. <u>I Michelangelo, Sculptor: An Autobiography Through Letters</u> ed. Irving and Jean Stone. (New York: New American Library of World Literature, 1964). A fascinating psychological and spiritual self-portrait materializes in this collection of letters and poems of Michelangelo to his family, friends, the Medici, popes, artists, and business associates.

Irwin Edman. <u>Arts and the Man</u> (New York: W. W. Norton, 1939). This book remains highly readable and relevant, an illuminating analysis by a major American philosopher of what art and the artist are and how they function to make civilization possible.

Betty Edwards. <u>Drawing on the Right Side of the Brain</u> (Los Angeles: J. P. Tarcher, 1979). Practical exercises for people who have never drawn and are convinced they can't draw.

Vincent van Gogh. <u>Dear Theo: The Autobiography of Vincent van Gogh</u>. ed. Irving Stone. (Garden City, N.Y.: Doubleday & Co., 1946). Vincent van Gogh's philosophy of life and art emerges in these poignant letters to his beloved brother, Theo.

H. W. Janson. <u>History of Art</u>, second edition. (Englewood Cliffs, N.J.: Prentice-Hall, Inc., 1977). A beautifully illustrated classic, which traces Western art from early cave paintings through the 1960s.

Dimitri Merejowski. <u>The Romance of Leonardo da Vinci</u> (New York: Modern Library, 1955). A fascinating fictionalized account of the life of Leonardo set against the background of the Renaissance.

Mary McCarthy. <u>The Stones of Florence</u> (New York: Harcourt Brace, 1959). A beautifully illustrated description of the past and present of the Italian city, often called a living museum.

Survey 1

1. In art, vertical lines express stability and order, while diagonal lines are useful in expressing

   1. motion.
   2. aggression.
   3. imbalance.
   4. chaos.
   5. dependency

2. Woodrow Tatlock, so goes the text, was most lacking in empathy. The best meaning of empathy would be which of the following?

   1. being charitable toward others
   2. enjoying a peak experience
   3. the ability to alienate oneself when necessary
   4. the ability to see beyond oneself
   5. the ability to relate significant events to one's own life.

3. Which of the following is NOT an assumption of education in the humanities?

   1. People come into the world fully prepared to live an enriched life.
   2. Human skills should not be employed solely for the good of industry or the state.
   3. Living is an art that must be learned.
   4. Humanity is an end in itself.
   5. People must be free to choose between significant alternatives.

4. In the TV program The Way of the Humanist, the little girl has a strong preference for which subject in school?

   1. mathematics
   2. geography
   3. physical science
   4. home economics
   5. poetry

5. All of the following are characteristics of an effective human life EXCEPT

    1. a strong loyalty to time-proven beliefs.
    2. changing one's life style when necessary
    3. willingness to feel and to show emotion.
    4. making the most of one's environment.
    5. reexamining one's beliefs periodically.

6. Which of the following statements best describes an attitude you hold toward the cultural resources of the area in which you live?

    1. There are very few cultural resources, and I wish there were more.
    2. There may or may not be ample cultural resources, but in either case I am not concerned.
    3. There are ample cultural resources, but I don't have time for them.
    4. There are ample cultural resources, and I take advantage of many of them.
    5. There are ample cultural resources, and I intend to take advantage of more of them.

7. Which of the following statements best summarizes Woodrow Tatlock's final attitude toward the Mona Lisa?

    1. "The painting does not deserve its fame."
    2. "I now see why people revere Leonardo's masterpiece."
    3. "It helps to look at the Mona Lisa with one eye closed."
    4. "An artist's mind is a beautiful thing, but not to me."
    5. "The Mona Lisa is generally admired because of its economic value."

8. Nelson Rockefeller and a Renaissance Pope had something in common. Which of the following best expresses what it was?

    1. They refused to be patrons of art.
    2. Each had a problem with a particular artist.
    3. Each believed he could paint better than a commissioned artist.
    4. Each exploited the talents of an artist for profit.
    5. Both have become more famous than the artists they supported.

9. Whereas van Gogh's emotional intensity was released through the varied brush-strokes and brilliant colors in this paintings, Michelangelo's could be felt in his

    1. distortion of the shapes of his subjects.
    2. use of the chiaroscuro effect.
    3. preference for the flexibility of the fresco.
    4. implanting in the marble a dynamic quality.
    5. choice of flawed, rather than perfect marble.

10. Why do you think the narrator of Art: Tell Me What I Am is compelled to paint on the blank wall?

    1. Because it's there.
    2. Because it was forbidden by law.
    3. He needed to put himself in the external world.

23

4. He enjoyed vandalism.
5. He knew that political propaganda could be hidden behind brushstrokes.

11. In your opinion, which of the following motivations best illustrates the meaning of <u>Divine Discontent</u>?

    1. Leonardo's dissatisfaction with payment received for the <u>Mona Lisa</u>
    2. Goya's dislike of country life and longing for Madrid
    3. Michelangelo's need to create a work worthy of God
    4. Beethoven's scorn for Baroque improvisations
    5. Van Gogh's insistence that creative purity and economic consideration are compatible

12. Using Aristotle's terminology, we can say that when an artist reproduces the creative process of nature, he or she is

    1. deviating
    2. expanding
    3. challenging
    4. imitating
    5. analyzing

13. <u>The Man With No Time For Beauty</u> makes one of the following suggestions to people if they would avoid having a retirement like Woodrow Tatlock's. Which is it?

    1. Everything you need is right in your own backyard.
    2. Surround yourself with your own personal culture.
    3. Act your age.
    4. Don't perceive everything through your own values.
    5. Married people should travel while they're young enough to enjoy each other.

14. Woodrow Tatlock the child appears to have had things that Woodrow Tatlock the adult has lost: imagination, creativity, openness to life. Which of the following reasons BEST explains that loss?

    1. the death of his wife
    2. his failure to become manager of the hardware store
    3. too many college courses
    4. a failure to travel
    5. a limited, mainly materialistic, set of goals

15. One pervasive characteristic of Rembrandt's art is

    1. a sharp contrast between light and shadow
    2. the use of human figures as geometric designs.
    3. short, stabbing brushstrokes, suggesting explosive energy.
    4. lonely landscapes, devoid of human beings.
    5. an excessive use of rose colors.

16. What did Woodrow have as a child that he lost as an adult?

    1. a sled named Rosebud

2. an uncontrollable temper
3. a love for classical music
4. a fear of traveling
5. an openness to life

17. The meaning of mime's hat and cane, like all symbols, is open to a variety of interpretations. Which of the following possible interpretations strikes you as the best?

    1. an escape from drab reality
    2. the intuitive approach to life
    3. the rational approach to life
    4. the idealistic approach to life
    5. There is no one "best" interpretation.

18. Perspective drawing was developed during the

    1. 18th century.
    2. Impressionist period.
    3. Gothic period.
    4. Renaissance.
    5. Post-Napoleonic era.

19. An invention that brought about a change in the nature and purpose of art was

    1. the woodcut.
    2. lithography.
    3. photography.
    4. phenomenology.
    5. acrylics.

20. In his Guernica mural, Pablo Picasso has given us a supreme example of cubism, a style of painting in which

    1. only square forms are permitted.
    2. the artist works entirely in contrasting shades of blue.
    3. there are pronounced differences between light and shadow.
    4. people and objects are transformed into geometric shapes.
    5. symbolism becomes more significant than design.

21. Of the following artists, which one painted the most evidently cynical works?

    1. Michelangelo
    2. Manet
    3. Goya
    4. Rembrandt
    5. Leonardo

22. The painter who worked in more styles and techniques than anyone in the history of art was

    1. Francisco Goya.
    2. Pablo Picasso.

3. Vincent van Gogh.
4. Sigmund Freud.
5. Claes Oldenburg.

23. A revolt against a set of rules, a new way of painting, a fresh look at nature, thick brushstrokes, and a concern for the artist's subjective states characterize the movement known as

    1. idealism.
    2. impressionism.
    3. realism.
    4. romanticism.
    5. chiaroscuro.

24. In sculpture, the stone _____ Michelangelo's chisel in much the same way that the canvas _____ the artist's brush. Which verb is appropriate for both statements?

    1. welcomes
    2. denies
    3. destroys
    4. resists
    5. mocks

25. Michelangelo and the Pope were in conflict over the frescoes in the Sistine Chapel. Which of the following versions of this conflict is most accurate?

    1. good taste vs. kitsch
    2. political radicalism vs. uninvolvement
    3. artistic integrity vs. the rights of those who pay the bill
    4. secular, even shocking, subject matter vs. spirituality
    5. the right of the artist to change history around vs. a respect for truth

26. About which of the following cultures would we know little or nothing if it were not for the art it left behind?

    1. Greek
    2. Islamic
    3. Mayan
    4. Sioux
    5. Ik

27. Of which artist can this be said? "Most of his great works exhibit bold brushstrokes, aggressive use of bright colors, and use of uninterrupted flowing energy--all reflective of his inner turmoil, from which he descended into madness and suicide."

    1. Rembrandt
    2. van Gogh
    3. Picasso
    4. Manet
    5. Michelangelo

28. The subject matter and appearance of Goya's later work raises a crucial question regarding the nature and purpose of art. Which question is it?

    1. whether propaganda can be art
    2. whether a work of art can be unpleasant to look at
    3. whether a work of art can be mystical
    4. whether an artist has a right to be mainly concerned with money
    5. whether an artist can strive to please his patron

29. The phrase <u>hemispheric asymmetry</u> meant that

    1. the East and the West have different value systems and therefore different esthetic ideals.
    2. the two halves of our brain can give us different ways of perceiving.
    3. prevailing ideas about the purpose of art in Communist Russia are radically different from those in Western democracies.
    4. in the normal person, the right side of the brain deals with logic, mathematics, and a concern with time.
    5. the left side of the brain deals with the Dionysian aspect of the self.

30. "There was a child went forth every day,
    And the first object he look'd upon, that object he became,
    And that object became part of him for the day or a certain part of the day,
    Or for many years or stretching cycles of years."

    Walt Whitman's lines are quoted in the text to illustrate an activity central to the visual arts. This activity is

    1. symbolization.
    2. use of perspective.
    3. minimalizing.
    4. abstracting.
    5. mimesis.

31. The cave art at Lascaux is presented as evidence that

    1. the early artists used their paintings to control nature by sympathetic magic.
    2. the need to imitate is older even than human language.
    3. the human tendency to symbolize produced the earliest examples of visual art.
    4. Paleolithic arts had an understanding of perspective.
    5. earliest societies used art in the service of religion.

32. The sculptor Edmonia Lewis is notable in the art world as

    1. a woman artist becoming an important cultural champion.
    2. the first Black American sculptor to become famous.
    3. the first artist to use steel as a medium for sculpture.
    4. 1 and 2.
    5. 2 and 3.

33. Tendencies of the Minimalist school of art appear in the work of

1. Pablo Picasso.
2. Claude Monet.
3. Georgia O'Keeffe
4. Salvador Dali.
5. Paul Klee.

34. An important change in the role of Black artists in the twentieth century is that

    1. they are patronized by wealthy philanthropists.
    2. they have become highly effective cultural champions.
    3. they have joined the ranks of artists alienated from middle class values.
    4. they have generally rejected their ethnic ties, believing them to inhibit free expression.
    5. 2 and 3.

MODULE III

Music, the Planned Environment

OVERVIEW

Music is the shaped sound between silences; it is humanity's defense against accidental, random noise and constitutes therefore the planned audio environment. No doubt music originated in humanity's efforts to imitate the pleasing sounds that existed naturally: the sounds of water, wind, or the song of a bird. But as musical tradition grew, the creators of these "shaped sounds" reached out for more and more unusual and complex combinations of sounds. Rhythm, harmony, dissonance, and improvisation added to melodic lines produced a rich variety of audio experience, enabling people to discover what their feelings sounded like. Very often, however, musical innovations are met with hostility as the expectations of listeners are thwarted. Contemporary music is characterized by a wide range of sounds, many of them extremely alien to ears accustomed to softer, more romantic tones. Since music enables us to achieve a heightened awareness of what we are like deep down inside, it follows that one should develop an attitude of openness and tolerance toward what may strike one at first as too unfamiliar to be acceptable.

LEARNING OBJECTIVES

Having completed this module, you should be able to

1) define the basic musical elements presented in the module.

2) present the theory of the first musical instrument.

3) summarize the critical opinion that musical achievement has nothing to do with personal taste.

4) show how certain rhythms tell us much about certain historical periods.

5) distinguish between melody in general, and the romantic notion of melody.

6) explain why it is unwise to limit one's tastes in music.

7) indicate characteristics of a Bach toccata or fugue, a Beethoven symphony, jazz, rock, folk music, and popular songs.

8) relate the forms and styles of Bach to the baroque tradition in music.

9) describe how Beethoven made use of the Haydn/Mozart tradition, but expanded the range of musical expression.

29

10) point out some similarities in the form of baroque music and modern jazz, focusing on considerations of freedom and form.

11) give reasons why contemporary music may sound unpleasant to some listeners.

12) give examples of some innovations in music that have met with resistance.

AS YOU READ

Chapter 2: "Music: Sound and Silence"

1. Why are passages of silence such important components of music?

2. Be able to define and give examples of the following musical elements: interval, pitch, rhythm, melody, timbre, and harmony.

3. What place does Plato give music in his ideal Republic?

4. Why is a waltz considered Apollonian music, while rock can be called Dionysian?

5. Does the definition "what emotions sound like" apply to all music, or only some music?

6. The chapter offers at least one way to evaluate a popular song. What is it?

7. What is a fugue? A toccata? In what period did these musical forms arise? What composer is noted for them?

8. Be able to summarize the achievements of the composer cited above.

9. Give examples of how folk music is used to release tensions, to create a feeling of group unity, to protest social conditions.

10. What place do Haydn and Mozart occupy in the history of music?

11. How did Beethoven both continue and expand the tradition established by Haydn and Mozart?

12. Give several examples of how innovations in music, just as in other arts, met with resistance when they first appeared. What forms do some of today's innovations take?

13. Why should you try to listen to music you don't like? Is it desirable to like more than one kind of music? Why? Why not?

VIEWING

I.   Sound to Music

--Cassandria Hanna, who plays most of the music for this program, is both a
teacher and prominent concert pianist. She is especially associated with the
Afro-American concert music tradition and has brought eminent black composers to
the attention of concert goers. In his professional life, Alfred Pinkston is an
academic administrator, but he enjoys working as a jazz pianist in his spare
time. Pinkston's life style offers a fine example of the humanist's multi-
leveled approach.

--Music is defined as the planned sound environment, as one means whereby humans
have been able to control the sounds amid which they live. Such control
inevitably leads to the possibility of <u>manipulation</u> through music. The Greeks,
for example, discovered that sending soldiers off to war with martial strains
ringing in their ears created more aggressive armies. Today we find many
examples of musical manipulation. Musak keeps factories, banks, offices,
restaurants, and airplanes from ever being silent. Background scores in motion
pictures channel the emotions of the viewer, forcing him to experience the
screen events in certain ways. Perhaps you can think of other instances of
music control.

--The suggestion has been made that rock music is good for deadening the
emotions. No doubt many disagree and argue that rock liberates the emotions.
Can a case be made for both points of view?

--Rhythm may be the most important single ingredient in musical experience
because its regular <u>punctuations</u> appear to satisfy a deep human need, a need
which is continually frustrated by the unrhythmic aspects of daily life.

--The most common kind of plainsong is the medieval Gregorian chant. There is
only the pure melody, sung without any harmony. It is almost impossible to tell
how many voices are singing these chants; the idea was that individuality is
unimportant on the spiritual level.

--In polyphony (or counterpoint), as opposed to the plainsong or monophonic
music, two melodies play against each other, forming a pleasing unity of sound.
The rise of polyphony began during the Renaissance, when the medieval deemphasis
on the individual was replaced by the glorification of personality and the
differences among human beings.

--In Beethoven, dissonance (two notes clashing against each other in a sound that
is not immediately pleasing) becomes just as important as harmony. Beethoven
seems to appreciate the fact that harmonious sounds do not allow for a complete
expression of inner feelings. His most characteristic musical principle -
dynamics - reflects the recognition that abrupt changes in intensity are also
necessary for complete expression.

--All music has melody, but the average listeners identify only certain combinations of notes as being "melodic." Modern composers of concert music deliberately avoid melodies that sound overly familiar. It is important to give

31

contemporary music a chance to identify itself before we reject it for sounding alien and sometimes even "unpleasant."

II. Jazz/Bach

--In the opening sequence we see a brook, a river, an ocean. These successively larger, more energetic bodies of water, represent a principle that is paralleled in the arts: that is, the artist seeks liberation (like the water in the ocean), but the urge toward freedom is always being countered by the limitations of the medium. The result is a dynamic tension, which is perhaps almost perfectly embodied in music.

--Bach and jazz have one major element in common: improvisation, the need of the music to take flight from the limitations of musical form. At the same time, we learn that liberation could not happen without the set musical form. This surely suggests that jazz musicians, masters at improvisation, are also well trained, skilled technicians, who have first mastered the forms they seek to depart from.

--The origins of jazz, in the late 19th century, can be found in the coming together of Afro-American sounds and musical energies and the more "polite" and structured European musical forms, such as the quadrille.

--Scott Joplin made jazz "respectable" in white supper clubs. For a time Joplin was popular and celebrated, as was Bach before him. Both composers, however, fell into oblivion before their deaths: Bach, because the new sounds of Haydn and Mozart were supplanting his Baroque sounds; Joplin, because his career pursued less and less popular forms, such as opera. (Joplin's opera Treemonisha has only recently been performed.)

--Louis Armstrong introduced the principle of jazz improvisation to combos of musicians. Charlie Parker contributed musical complexities and harmonies previously unheard in jazz. Duke Ellington took jazz into the concert hall with elaborate musical scores as well as improvisation.

--At the end of the program the term Jazz/Bach is introduced and defined as the musical expression of humanity's ongoing spirit of rebellion. But we must not forget that the term also suggests the balance between rebellion (improvisation) and structure (musical form). Each needs the other.

32

SELF-TEST

Match each item in the first column with an item in the second. Use no item more than once.

T	1.	silence	ragtime	_____
T	2.	Japanese music	reflects the Dionysian self	_____
VT	3.	fugue	jazz in the concert hall	_____
VT	4.	improvisation	experience in music is the highest kind of education	_____
V	5.	Duke Ellington		
V	6.	polyphony	necessary change from harmony	_____
			exists for the individual note	_____
T	7.	Napoleon		
T	8.	plainsong	shared by Bach and jazz players	_____
V	9.	dissonance	an Apollonian dance form	_____
			two melodies heard together	_____
VT	10.	Scott Joplin		
T	11.	Plato	disillusioned Beethoven after having inspired him	_____
T	12.	the Charleston	medieval musical form	_____
T	13.	the waltz	makes the basic elements of music possible	_____
T	14.	scoundrel song	developed with Renaissance	_____
			emphasis on individualism	_____
			Dionysian dance form of the 1920s	_____

CHECK LIST OF MAIN IDEAS

1. Music is significant sound shaped by silence.

2. Music as an art form constitutes the controlled or planned, as opposed to the unplanned or random, audio environment.

3. Music can be the external anchor of the feelings; through the ages it has been used to express, generate, intensify, identify, and soothe the emotions. But it can also exist as a pure art form without reference to emotions.

4. The fully realized person, by listening to great music of the past such as Mozart and Beethoven, can enrich her life; at the same time it is important to open one's ears to unfamiliar sounds of the modern period.

RECOMMENDED READING

Willi Apel. <u>Harvard Dictionary of Music</u> (Cambridge, Mass.: Harvard University Press, 1969).

Leonard Bernstein. <u>The Joy of Music</u> (New York: Simon and Shuster, 1959). The enthusiasm of this composer-conductor is conveyed to the page. Bernstein addresses the reader ("Now that you've heard what syncopation is like, let's see what...Blues would sound like without it") and makes provocative comparisons across the centuries.

Pablo Casals. <u>Joys and Sorrows</u> as told to Albert Kahn (New York: Simon and Shuster, 1970). The story of a great cellist's pursuit of beauty and justice and the famous people he encounters along the way.

Leon Dallin. <u>Listener's Guide to Musical Understanding</u> (including record set). Dubuque, Iowa: W.C. Brown, 1977.

Donald Grout. <u>History of Western Music</u> (New York: W.W. Norton & Co., 1973).

Charles Ives. <u>Essays Before a Sonata and Other Writings</u> (New York: W.W. Norton, 1961). In this series of essays a celebrated American composer discusses the nature of music as well as the sources of his impulses and inspiration.

Le Roi Jones. <u>Blues People</u> (New York: William Morrow, 1967). A penetrating examination of the philosophy of black music and how it reflects the black experience in America.

Romaine Rolland. <u>Beethoven</u> (Freeport, N.Y.: Books for Libraries Press, 1969). A classic biography of the composer by a novelist of major stature.

RECOMMENDED LISTENING

Concert Music

Johann S. Bach. <u>Toccata and Fugue in D for Organ</u>, E. Power Biggs, organ. Columbia, #M-32933.

Ludwig van Beethoven. <u>Symphony No. 9 in D</u>, Opus 125, "Choral," Berlin Philharmonic, Fricsay conducting. Deutsch-Grammaphon #2525203. <u>Sonata No. 29 in B flat</u>, Opus 106, "Hammerklavier," Rudolf Serkin, Piano. Columbia, #M-10081.

Franz Joseph Haydn. <u>Symphony No. 96 in D</u>, "Miracle," St. Martin's Academy Orchestra, Marriner conducting. Phillips #9500348.

Wolfgang A. Mozart. <u>Symphony No. 41 in C</u>, K 551, "Jupiter," English Chamber Orchestra, Barenboim conducting. Angel #S-36761.

_____. <u>Don Giovanni</u>, K 527, (opera based on the Don Juan legend) Shwarzkopf, Sutherland, Wachter, Taddei singing with the Philadelphia Orchestra. Angel #S-3605.

Petr Ilich Tchaikovsky. Overture to Romeo and Juliet, New York Philharmonic, Bernstein conducting. Columbia #MS-6014.

Richard Wagner, excerpts from Tristan and Isolde (including the "Liebestod"), Nilssen, Ludwig, Wingassen singing with the Bayreuth Festival Orchestra. Deutsch-Grammophon #2713301.

Blues and Jazz

Louis Armstrong and the Dukes of Dixieland. Definitive Album. Audio Fidelity #6241.

Chick Corea and Gary Burton. Crystal Silence. ECM/Polydor #1024.

Duke Ellington. Greatest Hits. Reprise #6234.

Bessie Smith. World's Greatest Blues Singer. Columbia #CG-33.

Jimmy Yancey, Earl Hines, Art Tatus, et al. A Jazz Piano Anthology. Columbia #PG-32355.

Folk

Libba Cotton. Shake Sugaree. Folkways #31003E

Pete Seeger. American Favorite Ballads. Folkways #31017E.

Gospel

Mahalia Jackson. In Concert. Columbia #CS 9490.

Ragtime

Scott Joplin. Music of Scott Joplin. Scott Joplin, piano. Biograph #1013.

MODULE IV

Drama and Film

(NOTE: This Module is composed of Chapters 3 and 4 of the text, dealt with
separately. There are no video programs to accompany Chapter 4.)

OVERVIEW - DRAMA

Tragedy and comedy are the major forms of dramatic art, surviving from age to
age with an obvious capacity for filling deep rooted psychological needs. More than
passing entertainments, they represent aspects of the human personality and fundamental attitudes toward what happens to us during our lives. There are times when we
are appallingly surrounded by disastrous events and have no choice but to see life as
tragic. But, fortunately, there are other times when we have to laugh--at ourselves
--and others for all of the nonsense we human beings are guilty of doing and
believing. Whether we should weep or laugh all of the time is open to question, but
one thing seems clear: the person who cannot do either one is somehow missing the
chance to maintain a psychological balance.

LEARNING OBJECTIVES

Having completed this module, you should be able to

1) describe the nature and characteristics of major works in tragic and comic
   art.

2) describe the nature and purposes of tragedy as a form of dramatic art.

3) summarize Aristotle's theory of tragedy.

4) contrast the classical and modern tragic protagonist.

5) define the fundamental nature of comedy in comparison with and in contrast
   to that of tragedy.

6) describe tragic and comic attitudes as resources for living.

7) show how a contemporary dramatist might create a classical tragedy about a
   contemporary figure.

8) relate Willie Loman, protagonist of Arthur Miller's Death of a Salesman, to
   the circumstances Aristotle designated as appropriate to the protagonist in
   tragic drama.

9) using King Lear and Othello, summarize the nature and fate of the
   Shakespearean tragic hero.

10) identify both comic and tragic qualities in Charlie Chaplin's characteriza-
    tion of the Little Tramp.

11) discuss the importance of free choice as a factor in classical and modern tragedy.

AS YOU READ

Chapter 3: "Two Masks"

1. We could say that both tragedy and comedy make life easier to bear. Contrast the ways in which they do it.

2. A major difference between classical and modern tragic heroes is class. Explain.

3. Contrast the two major forms of tragic irony. Give an example of each.

4. Contrast either Oedipus or King Lear with Blanche DuBois as tragic protagonists. Why would some critics say that Blanche is not tragic?

5. Be able to list and describe some enduring comic types. Can you find examples in contemporary comedies such as M*A*S*H?

6. Summarize the achievements of Moliere on the comic stage. What makes his plays survive?

7. Comedies tend to be about knaves, fools, and rogues. Indicate the characteristics of each. What examples can you find in dramas?

8. What justification can be made for the viewpoint that the funniest comedies are often the most serious. Give some examples.

9. What could one say to a person who insists that life's tragic side is too awful to face, and one should laugh as often and as long as possible? Or to a person who believes that life is too serious for laughter?

10. Identify the Commedia dell' Arte elements that appear in TV sit-coms.

11. Characterize the rogue hero and explain why the audience doesn't despise him.

12. What influences in the twentieth century have affected the kind of things we laugh at?

13. Why is it important for the audience to have a commonly shared knowledge of the plot circumstances if Sophoclean irony is to work? Find an example of a Shakespearean soliloquy that prepares the audience for Sophoclean irony.

14. The statement is made that great comedies are possible only in times that give priority to rationality over sentimentality and that permit audiences to laugh at folly--even in high places. Do you consider that you are living in such an era?

VIEWING

I. The Tragic Vision

--The general view of the tragic experience presented in this program is that
suffering and growth go hand in hand. Without tragedy in human life, people
would not learn, would not be forced to cope. In a paradoxical sense, then,
tragedy really is a blessing in disguise. Woe to that person whose life seems
to be perpetually spared. Sooner or later he will find himself overwhelmed. It
is better to face the tragic side of life while one has many resources for
dealing with it.

--"When the gods created man, they allotted to him death." Whether we turn to
the Gilgamesh story, or to the story of the Garden of Eden and the many other
accounts people have left to explain the meaning of existence, the message is
always the same: "People must die." This fact colors and conditions every
aspect of our lives. It is the ultimate source and cause of tragic experience,
which, it cannot be said often enough, is not limited to theatrical dramas.

--One other truth which this universal story of Gilgamesh recognizes is the flaw
perceived to exist at the heart of creation. Something, human instinct has
always told us, is wrong with the moral order of things, or perhaps it is that
no such moral order is there at all. But human beings still believe there is,
or ought to be. Human beings have visions of perfection. For this reason
reality continues to frustrate and to shock. (But our reaction can be comic as
well as tragic.)

--One cannot stress often enough the profoundly tragic character of that Greek
masterwork the Iliad. No one can be said to understand the Greeks if he has not
understood the essence of this poem. He won't understand the full meaning of
tragic vision either. The Iliad offers that vision in dozens of moving epi-
sodes. Take, for example, the death of the Trojan hero Hector. Hector is the
most noble, most admirable of all the heroes in the epic--Greek or Trojan. But
he is human, whereas, in his final combat, his opponent is the half-god
Achilles. The two are alone outside the walls of Troy. Hector knows what the
odds are; nevertheless, he chooses to stand. Suddenly, his brother Deiphobus
appears at his side--rather, the form of Deiphobus appears, for it is really
Athena in his guise, having come to assure Achilles's victory. Hector,
heartened by what he believes to be unexpected aid, flings his spear at the foe.
It misses, and now he reaches back for the spear that Deiphobus will hand him.
Deiphobus is gone; only thin air fills the space where he stood. Hector sees
now how the gods have tricked him and have decided his fate.

--In the Greek vision, tragedy has two sources. One, illustrated by the conquest
of Hector, sees humanity as the tragic victim of the way the universe works, in
this case represented by the cruel superpower of the gods. The other source of
tragedy is the flaw in humanity itself. Both are supremely illustrated in the
masterwork of Sophocles, Oedipus the King, an excerpt from which is performed by
the narrator. As the legend of Oedipus shows, the hero's destiny was decided
even before his birth, and it is a disastrous one. He has no choice but one day
to kill his father and marry his mother. To this extent he is a victim of the
tragic nature of things, once again symbolized by the outrageous power of the
gods. On the other hand, the play of Oedipus is not really about a man who

39

kills his father and marries his mother, but rather about a man who persistently denies reality. He is told by the prophet Teiresias what he has done, and he insists Teiresias is lying. The flaw in the universe has its counterpart in human character. Oedipus has all of the noble qualities one would want a king to possess, but he lacks the all-important quality of objectivity. Like most ordinary mortals, the king who would be supreme tries to live in terms of his own version of truth, and the effort is what destroys him.

--Though many would agree that Hamlet is the "world's greatest play," the reasons are not always easy to find. Like many of the noblest works of the human imagination, Hamlet is an original, not a type. It is a whole irreducible to the sum of its parts. Consequently, people disagree over what makes Hamlet a tragedy. One view, suggested by the host/narrator, is that the play is a tragedy about the loss of idealism--that of the romantic youth who suddenly finds himself face to face with the sordid and terrible truth behind appearances. Unhappy as it may be, the passage from youthful innocence to pessimistic maturity is as universal as any theme found in tragedy.

--King Lear, called Shakespeare's most monumental tragedy, has a scope and a breadth of wisdom that also defy total analysis. Nonetheless, its ancient hero's tragic flaw seems evident. He has been a king for too long, and he takes his omnipotence for granted. He has forgotten what it is to be an ordinary mortal, but mortal he is. The work has assumed even more relevance for its parallels with contemporary personalities: people who have been in power too long, people who claim executive privilege, people who cannot empathize with the powerless and hungry. But in his dotage, Lear loses all freedom of will, is manipulated by his power-hungry daughters, and so suggests another contemporary theme: the dehumanization of human beings as they become pawns in the interplay of forces (nations, corporations, political games) which they cannot even comprehend, much less control.

--But taken as a whole, the tragic tradition in human culture rests upon an assumption of free will (though, as we have seen, the absence of freedom can also be a tragic theme). The narrator sums up the presentation by calling tragedy perhaps "our most precious possession," because, even if the hero fails, he or she has been free to fail. (Oedipus, for example, faced with the truth of his past, is free to accept or to reject it.) The persistence of tragedy as an art form and the tragic outlook on life seem to offer proof that humanity is free; otherwise how could there be so much failure?

II. Knaves and Fools

--Sam Hirsch points out that the gift of humor springs from a serious view of life. The word "serious" is used here as a synonym for "rational." In other words, the comic writer or performer, as well as the individual who possesses a true sense of humor, begins with certain rational expectations regarding human events and behavior. When these are violated (when there is an irrational turn of events or when someone behaves in an irrational manner), laughter comes to the rescue and prevents frustration, even despair. Some of the most brilliant humanists (such as Jonathan Swift and Mark Twain) have been more than a little cynical, but humor has enabled them to maintain a sense of balance.

--"When life is viewed as a tragedy," says Hirsch, "there is still some dignity left." In comedy very often things go from bad to worse, and a situation utterly deteriorates until it is beyond tears. But the shadow of tragedy may still be lurking in the background. The host makes reference to the clown who slips on the banana peel. We laugh because there can no longer be any question of human dignity; yet--stop to think of it--the situation can be very close to tragic disaster.

--"Christendom was crawling with knaves, fools, and hypocrites" when Swift picked up his pen to retaliate. Where other people of the Church might have responded to the general corruption through scathing sermons on vice, Swift chose the way of the satirist. Gulliver's Travels, which many readers have always regarded as no more than a delightful children's fantasy, pokes less than gentle fun at pretentiousness, greed, and depravity.

--"A Modest Proposal" (1729) has long remained Swift's single most admired piece of writing, a satiric essay nearly perfect in intention and execution. The method of satire employed as a means of lashing out at the English maltreatment of the Irish is called Swiftian irony. The technique is simple: instead of outwardly condemning the English attitude toward the Irish, the author writes as if he were an English country squire, appalled by the poverty in Ireland and, ostensibly, desirous of suggesting a solution to the problem. However, the solution--eat the children of the poor--is so outrageous that, in addition to being grimly funny, it utterly destroys the English position. Ever since Swift, satirists have devastated their opposition by pretending to support it but, in the process, greatly exaggerating its faults.

--Satire, as Hirsch points out, is one form of humor. It is the most moralistic, the form most pointedly dedicated to effecting a real change. Ever since Aristophanes fathered comedy in Athens thousands of years ago, societies have had their professional satirists: self-appointed guardians of sanity in the midst of what they see as a world gone mad (and usually they're right!). Don Wright, a Pulitzer Prize winning political cartoonist, is one such guardian for our time. Can you think of others?

--Joan Rivers, a popular comic on television and in night clubs, regards herself as one such satirist/guardian. She expresses the opinion that the climate has become favorable for serious, biting humor in the United States since the Watergate scandal and public outrage over the suppression of so many vital facts. In her view, the serious humorist is one unbeatable source of public understanding. Still, there are many who believe that humor is currently at a low ebb in this country. They maintain that, in order to have great humor there must be a relatively stable society and a common value system. Do you agree?

--Charlie Chaplin's "Little Tramp" characterization has the simplicity shared by many great works of art. At the same time, one finds it difficult to analyze the technique. Often he attempts to be the knave, trying to pull a fast one wherever possible (e.g., in the Mission scene). In the classic tradition of comedy, the knave hero usually outrages us by his flagrant disregard for moral custom, but we admire him because he lives out our own antisocial fantasies. We generally laugh not at him but at the fools he manages to delude. Charlie's Tramp, however, is both knave and fool. Though he may get the better of the big bully, the City will always engulf him in the end. Most of Charlie's fadeouts have the Tramp making his comic way down a long street with the buildings of the City towering above. His efforts to be the suave, knowledgeable man of the world are always seen in perspective finally, and he ends up as the universal Little Man. Charlie's fame thus rests upon the singular achievement of having reached dead center between the comic and the near-tragic. Since a well rounded existence requires a sensitivity to both sides of life, we can say that Charlie Chaplin "did it all."

SELF-TEST

Match each item in the first column with an item in the second. Use no item more than once.

T	1.	defined the tragic hero as both high-born and flawed	Euripidean irony _____
T	2.	audience knows; character doesn't	most moralistic form of humor _____
VT	3.	youth dies; old age survives.	"Modest Proposal" _____
			single-mindedness _____
T	4.	common-man tragedy	King Lear _____
V	5.	satire	Gilgamesh _____
T	6.	flaw in many comic characters	Aristotle _____
V	7.	often called "the world's greatest play"	insisted on own version of reality _____
T	8.	catharsis	psychological purgation from tragedy _____
VT	9.	perhaps the earliest tragedy known	Willy Loman _____
VT	10.	Oedipus	Sophoclean irony _____
V	11.	suggestion that babies would make good roasts	Hamlet _____
			rogue hero _____
V	12.	dehumanized by too much power	
T	13.	Falstaff	

CHECK LIST OF MAIN IDEAS

1. Tragedy and comedy often explore similar themes, but the treatment of them (e.g. the frailty of human nature, life's ironies) varies.

2. Comedy maintains a distance between the characters and the audience - we laugh at rather than empathize with the protagonists, whereas in tragedy, we often identify with and usually feel compassion for the tragic hero.

3. Comic figures are generally stereotyped, displaying only one or a few personality facets and possessing "a comic flaw, single-mindedness."

4. While modern tragedians have departed from their earlier counterparts in that they tend to portray a common-man rather than the highly-born, both classical and modern tragedies observe some of the same conventions. The downfall of the protagonist often results from an inability to see things as they are.

5. A sense of the tragic and the comic is vital to the fully realized human being. Tragedy helps us to cope with life's disappointments and frustrations; comedy helps us to see the irrationality in others and ourselves.

OVERVIEW - FILM

The motion picture, a comparatively new genre, has become one of the world's wealthiest industries as well as an art form. It is sometimes said that the kind of commercial reward reaped by those involved in film production is incompatible with artistic integrity, the money tempting the artist to pander to popular tastes at the cost of creative vision. Nevertheless, as the text demonstrates, a number of notable films have made a great deal of money without sacrificing artistic excellence. This unit examines some of the motion pictures that are considered landmarks of the film industry; points out advances in film art achieved by new technology as well as by the genius of great directors; and discusses the particular talents that have given some directors and actors justifiable and probably permanent renown. It is sometimes asked whether a genre as recent as the motion picture ought to be classed with dramatic works whose reputations have survived millennia. Yet one of the premises we keep coming back to in this course is that an openness to new kinds of creative expression—as well as to the treasures of the past—is essential to anyone who would make the most of living.

LEARNING OBJECTIVES

Having completed this module, you should be able to

1) identify some major milestones in the history of film making.

2) give examples of cinematic techniques developed in the silent films.

3) explain what Charlie Chaplin's creation, the "Little Tramp," contributed to the sophistication of film art.

4) show how personae developed by actors like Cary Grant and Humphrey Bogart influenced the success of the films they appeared in.

5) give examples of the ways in which cinematic techniques employed in Gone with the Wind, Potemkin, and Citizen Kane can convey the director's ideas to the audience.

6) evaluate the theory that says the artist must choose between art and wealth.

7) explain the recent theory of auteurism relative to film art.

Chapter 4: "The Motion Picture: Art and Industry"

1. The motion picture gives us the illusion of continuous sight. Explain.

2. What contributions to the beginning film industry were made by George Mèliés? Thomas Edison? Marcus Loew?

3. The statement is made that Edwin S. Porter's introduction of the "cut" revolutionized the film industry. In what way? What other innovations is Porter credited with?

4. Explain the effect of the "lingering take" introduced by D.W. Griffith in Birth of a Nation.

5. In Mack Sennett comedies characters are subjected to dehumanizing abuse. How did Sennett keep the viewers from taking these catastrophes too seriously?

6. Charlie Chaplin learned from Mack Sennett's movie art and then went beyond it. What dimensions did Chaplin add to the comic figure?

7. Be able to show correspondences between popular film themes and events such as the Great Depression.

8. Lenin saw that the film medium had great potential for propaganda in Soviet Russia. In what ways did Sergei Eisenstein achieve and yet transcend successful propaganda in Potemkin?

9. What artistic advances were made in the "screwball" comedies of the thirties? Describe this genre and account for the fact that it has all but disappeared.

10. The text makes the point that films can have an effect on audiences that novels do not. How are such effects created in Citizen Kane and Gone with the Wind?

11. Relate the artistic success of Casablanca to the statement: "The great screen personae are examples of myth archetypes." Give some examples of memorable personae from your own experience of films.

12. What is there in the body of his work that entitles Alfred Hitchcock to be designated as an auteur?

13. Ingmar Bergman is described as a philosopher/film maker. From what you have read about The Seventh Seal and Wild Strawberries, can you perceive a persistent vision underlying the concrete terms of the films?

14. Casablanca and Citizen Kane are considered to be fine screen art for the same reasons. They can be contrasted in the way they achieved their reputation. Explain.

15. The designation of auteur is also given to directors such as Orson Welles and Ingmar Bergman. What traits make the work of these men recognizable?

SELF-TEST

Match each item in the first column with an item in the second. Use no item more than once.

1. penny arcade peep show   achieved status in screwball comedy _____

2. Edwin S. Porter   existential film maker _____

3. Charlie Chaplin   first major movie star _____

4. Orson Welles   elongated moment _____

5. Potemkin   artistic success achieved through persona of star _____

6. Katherine Hepburn

      sight gags _____

7. Mack Sennett

      introduced the "cut" _____

8. Ingmar Bergman

      American auteur _____

9. Casablanca

      first motion picture epic _____

10. Birth of a Nation

      Thomas Edison _____

CHECK LIST OF MAIN IDEAS

1. Commercialism is often believed to be an enemy to true artistic expression. However, while the motion picture has proved to be one of the most profitable forms of creative expression, some of the most financially successful movies are at the same time regarded as fine artistic achievements.

2. The silent film should not be regarded as a primitive form of entertainment. In that genre geniuses like Charlie Chaplin, D. W. Griffith, and Sergei Eisenstein developed a purely cinematic art form that achieved as much stature as great art in any other genre.

3. With artistic advances in the use of sound came improvement in the quality of dialog, a quality that has since waned as audience interest shifted from verbal wit to brilliant sound and visual effects made possible by technology.

4. Some highly artistic motion pictures owe their excellence to teamwork; others are the creations of directors who leave the imprint of their philosophy and style on the whole body of their work. These directors are sometimes called auteurs.

MASKS: THE KINSHIP OF TRAGEDY AND COMEDY

by

Donald M. Early

Sometimes we will say of a situation: "This would be funny if it weren't so tragic." Sometimes it is the other way round; we think: "This really is tragic, I suppose; but it's all so grotesque and improbable that I want to laugh." Each of us knows these ambivalent moments, when our emotions stand perplexed between two extremes. They seem to occur to remind us again how thin a line separates the tragic and the comic in human life.

The truth is, though we do on occasion recognize the ambivalent relationship of tragedy and comedy, our habit is to think of them as polarities, opposites, as separate masks experience chooses to wear--now one, now the other--to personify the darker and lighter aspects of the human drama. Objective truth, however, perceives a much more intimate, subtle, and troubling relationship between the two; and here seems the proper place for us to examine that relationship more closely.

> "To know what is serious
> we must also know what
> is laughable."
>
> --Socrates

We begin with tragedy. The tragedy in life is death. We all know that we must die; this inescapable conclusion permeates the whole of human existence and gives it its sombre undertone. It is a thing that cannot be laughed away; it is there. So we begin with that.

If death supplies the ground-base of existence, then the life force is its melody; and the product of their harmonies, their total music, is what concerns us here: the Largo and the Scherzo.

The Greeks, who invented the art form of tragedy, never assumed that tragedy told the whole story. They required that each tragic presentation be followed by a comedy, or satyr play, that made irreverent fun of the sombre events just enacted. The satyr play said: "Yes, yes, all that is so, and it's grave indeed; but it's funny too. Those pompous gods strutting about, treating men like flies, those blustering heroes daring fate to do its worst! Why all this self-importance? Why can't they relax, enjoy their ambrosia, or their beans and garlic, and make love, and have a good sleep?"

There is nothing in life, or art--or religion, for that matter--that does not also have its comic side. During the Middle Ages, at Carnival time, Christian worshipers celebrated something they called the Ass's Mass. It took place in church, before the altar, where an ass was made to officiate at this most sacred rite. A parody of the Mass was sung, and the faithful brayed their responses: "Hee haw!"

Blasphemous, surely! But it was not thought so, nor was it intended to be. It simply acknowledged that men were but fools in the eyes of God...that nothing that miserable humans could do, even in the service of God, was free from sin and the ludicrous. The Ass's Mass served to set man's state in proper perspective, and the comic view of life does it all the time.

William Hazlitt reminds us: "It is a common mistake to suppose that parodies degrade or imply a stigma on the subject; on the contrary, they in general imply something serious or sacred in the originals."

Comedy admires the noble truths of tragedy. It only asks to be allowed to comment as cogently, sharply, even painfully, as needed, in order that the whole truth can emerge and be confirmed. Sometimes, however, comedy cuts so close to the bone of the serious that the truth is too painful to accept. Since it won't go away, it must be subtly transformed, its features made to express what we want them to. Such enforced transformations can be observed in the case of certain works of art whose original intention made people uncomfortable. Chekhov's plays are an example. Chekhov wrote what he insisted were comedies. No one, however, wanted to see them that way: not directors, or critics, or audiences; the plays were "tragic." Now it is true that the characters in Chekhov's major plays do see themselves as tragic-- but they aren't; and that was exactly Chekhov's point. They are poor, bumbling fools who get themselves into ruinous tangles through their own misapprehensions. But so do we, in real life. When this truth is exposed, we choose to ignore it, and to see the whole muddle as noble suffering.

Or take the case of Schubert's "Serenade,"--one of the best-loved songs in music. We are told that Schubert wrote it somewhat with tongue in cheek, depicting with gentle amusement the extravagant passion of the lovelorn swain. To us latter-day romantics, however, the song isn't at all like that; we hear in its aching strains the very soul of love's longing.

Something similar has occurred with one of Mozart's songs. In the opera Cosi Fan Tutti, two male characters, bereft of their sweethearts, sing of their yearning in a duet. One of the lovers, however, is hungry, and images of food and love get mixed up in the number. The situation invites our laughter. But so beautiful is the music, so meltingly, yearningly sweet, that we cannot respond to it as comedy. We may be moved--to tears, perhaps, but never to laughter.

"Something inside of comedy isn't funny," says Walter Kerr. That "something" is what probes our weaknesses, exposing our peccadilloes and crimes. It also seems bent on exposing our gross subservience to our body's demands--the grumbling stomach, the nagging thirst, the involuntary erection, the need to defecate--even though we try to pretend we're "above" those things. Comedy loves to haul up our bestial origins, our vulnerability, our very mortality for inspection. "Here's what you really are," it says. But often there is no rejoicing on comedy's part. It would rather not have seen the truth; it turns aside--sadly.

Probably nowhere is comedy's ambivalence more clearly epitomized than in the complex image of the clown. The clown, at first glance, seems a figure designed for unalloyed laughter. He has a funny painted face that masks his true features; he

50

wears a ludicrous assortment of hand-me-downs; indulges in slapstick, plays the fall-guy shamelessly, is scorned, kicked, tricked, and beaten till he weeps. All of which we think marvelously funny, because thank God, he isn't us. He isn't our kind, but a different breed, and we can safely make him the butt of our jokes, the scape-goat for our embarrassing failures. Being "outside," he doesn't matter to those "inside."

But something then enters the picture here. The fact that the clown is outside puts him in position to view, with disturbing clarity, the actions of those on the inside. God, too, it must be remembered, judges from "outside." So we have to look carefully at what the clown's antics are saying. His crudeness and obscenity--do they pointedly comment on our own? Does he ape us in order to illustrate our own apishness? Is his slyness aimed at exposing our duplicities? When he plays the wretch and whipping boy, is he not acting out our own ignoble self-pity when we think ourselves victims of a malicious universe?

On the other hand, isn't the clown's dog-like love for the beautiful bareback rider, his hopeless dream of enfolding that tinseled loveliness in his arms--isn't that telling us, also, that he understands our impossible desire for the ideal, and shares our despair? Doesn't it seem that at heart he, too, yearns for the beauty, the truth, the perfection that humankind envisions?

Marcel Marceau, the famous French mime, does a scene of a man trying on a series of masks. No actual masks are used, of course; he does it all with that marvelously expressive painted face. One by one he tries them on and removes them, till the comic mask is donned. It won't come off. Embarrassed attempts, then desperate struggles fail. Finally, the truth sinks in, displaying only the agony of the man behind the mask--an agony that will go on and on...

Something of this tragic predicament is the clown's. The artist Georges Roualt, who painted such moving, suffering Christs in his stark, stained glass manner, also painted clowns that were even more shattering in their impact. Another painter, a contemporary named Jonah Kinigstein, has done a work he calls "Christ Among the Clowns." It shows the crucified Savior and two grotesque figures flanking the cross. Their clawlike hands reach toward the lacerated flesh. In anger, derision, suffering, love? It must be love--all the wretched, warped, and despairing love of the world, caught in one terrible tragic-comic moment: both mystery and revelation.

Apparently it is this kind of epiphany that certain Christian churches are now seeking by introducing the concept of "God's Fool" into their services. A lay group that calls itself "Clowns for Christ," made up mostly of young people, uses painted faces, mime, and music routines to teach the gospel lessons. Though this kind of evangelism may strike many people as strange, it is not new--as we know from our medieval account. Its very strangeness is doubtless its strength, perhaps jolting people into a new perception of life, where the visions of tragedy and comedy can merge in a single message.

RECOMMENDED READING

Aristophanes. The Clouds (Appears in various translations and editions). A satire which pokes fun at intellectuals and their endeavors.

_____. Lysistrata (Appears in various translations and editions). A classic satire on the war between nations and the war between the sexes.

Aristotle. Poetics (Appears in various translations and editions). The first known piece of literary criticism, containing Aristotle's famous definition of tragedy and the tragic hero.

Henri Bergson. "Laughter" in Comedy edited by Wylie Sypher (Garden City, N.Y.: Doubleday & Co., 1956). The respected metaphysician deals with laughter as humanity's way of restoring equilibrium in the presence of the irrational and the outrageous.

Cleanth Brooks, John G. Burser and Ribert Penn Warren. An Approach to Literature, 5th edition (Englewood Cliffs, N.J.: Prentice-Hall, Inc., 1976). An anthology which includes very good introductions to the elements of drama (pp 541-545).

Bosley Crowther. The Great Films (New York: Putnam's, 1967). A wonderfully illustrated analysis of fifty of the greatest films of all time, selected by the former New York Times movie critic.

_____. The Lion's Share (New York: Dutton, 1957). A fascinating historical panorama of the early days of film, centering on the development of the Metro-Goldwyn-Mayer empire.

Gilgamesh tr. Herbert Mason (New York: New American Library, 1970). The national epic of the ancient Babylonians, dealing with universal themes of human existence.

Homer. The Iliad. The epic poem which describes the fall of Troy.

Arthur Knight. The Liveliest Art (New York: Mentor Books, 1957). A leading scholar of film as an art form traces with particular depth the early years of the movies.

Gerald Mast. A Short History of the Film (New York: Pegasus, 1971). A readable account of milestones in film history, with emphasis on the esthetic achievements of great directors.

Arthur Miller. Death of a Salesman (New York: Viking Press, 1949). The prototype of the contemporary common-man tragedy.

Molier. The Miser tr. H. Baker and J. Miller (London: Dent, 1962). The 17th century comedy by France's greatest comic genius fully demonstrates that single mindedness is humanity's major comic flaw.

Friedrich Nietzsche. The Birth of Tragedy tr. Francis Golffing (Garden City, N.Y.:
Doubleday & Co., 1956). Nietzsche's study of tragedy is probably the most
significant since that of Aristotle, and in it he attacks the traditional
Aristotelian view that the moral (i.e. Apollonian) element is the most important
aspect in a tragedy. Nietzsche would have us appreciate the Dionysian qualities
(those which arouse passion and excitement) in tragedy as well as in the other
arts.

Ralph Rosenblum and Robert Karen. When the Shooting Stops...the Cutting Begins
(New York: Viking Press, 1979). The definitive work on the art of film
editing, presented chronologically with in-depth analyses of the great
achievements of this art.

William Shakespeare. King Lear (Appears in various editions). The story of the
victimization of an aging king by his vicious daughters; a fine example of
Euripidean irony.

Sophocles. Oedipus the King (Appears in various translations and editions). Many
critics believe this play to be the finest work of the Greek theatre, in
addition to having the world's most nearly perfect plot.

Jonathan Swift. The Portable Swift ed. Carl Van Doren (New York: Viking Press,
1964). A collection of Swift's most notable satires containing "A Modest
Proposal" and Gulliver's Travels.

Oscar Wilde. The Importance of Being Earnest (Great Neck, N.Y.: Barrons
Educational Series, 1959). A Victorian comedy of manners with perhaps the
wittiest dialog ever written.

SURVEY 2

1. The passage marked <u>marcia funebre</u> in Beethoven's <u>Eroica</u> is famous for the emotional power of

    1. the timpani roll.
    2. the stirring martial tempo.
    3. the silent pauses between musical phrases.
    4. the unexpected interjection of medieval plainsong.
    5. the introduction of counterpoint.

2. Brahms' First Symphony illustrates the point made in Chapter 2 that

    1. Brahms deserved more critical acclaim than he received in his own time.
    2. great composers fared better under the patronage of royalty than they do under the free enterprise system.
    3. Brahms' symphonies lack unity of theme and emotion.
    4. in music a pause can intensify the significance of what follows it.
    5. Brahms introduced improvisation into classical music.

3. Dionysian rhythm is present in

    1. the waltz.
    2. ragtime.
    3. square dance.
    4. the samba.
    5. rock.

4. Chapter 2 of the text advances the theory that the final movement of Beethoven's <u>Ninth Symphony</u> is attributed to the composer's

    1. belief that the orchestra alone could not express the gamut of feelings that he had to express.
    2. disenchantment when Napoleon demanded to be made emperor.
    3. deafness, which made it impossible for him to detect dissonance.
    4. failure to comprehend the limitations on the range of the human voice.
    5. return to the symphonic style of Haydn and Mozart.

5. The baroque music of Johann Sebastian Bach was unique in its time because of the use of

    1. harmony.

2. arrhythmic beat.
3. dissonance.
4. improvisation.
5. the human voice.

6. Scott Joplin is memorable for his ragtime, a musical genre marked by

   1. an Apollonian slow beat.
   2. sensuous themes, focusing on emotional states.
   3. lack of a definite melody.
   4. dissonant chords.
   5. Dionysian freedom from musical form.

7. In the fugue one hears

   1. the simultaneous use of different melodies.
   2. a single musical voice.
   3. a purely dissonant form.
   4. the simultaneous use of many rhythms.
   5. the commemoration of an important historical event.

8. Oedipus Rex is based on a myth about a king who has unknowingly killed his father and married his mother. The program The Tragic Vision points out, however, that the real tragedy in Sophocles' version of the story is that of a man who

   1. marries his mother for power not for love.
   2. sins against the gods by disobeying the prophecy.
   3. remains stubbornly blind to reality.
   4. disowns his children after discovering they were incestuously begotten.
   5. neglects his kingly duties in order to assist an old friend, thus exposing his country to grave danger.

9. In order for comedy to be effective, the situations and many of the characters as in the successful TV series M*A*S*H, must be viewed in terms of

   1. the ratings, which determine audience preferences.
   2. the classical requirements for comedy originally set forth by Aristophanes.
   3. what is actually going on in society at the time.
   4. the viewer's own prejudices, which comedy will basically affirm.
   5. a norm of underlying common sense.

10. The program The Tragic Vision pointed out that all of the great tragic heroes had something in common, and your text adds that modern attempts at tragedy often fail because the modern tragic hero is lacking in this supremely important characteristic, which is

    1. free will.
    2. intelligence.
    3. strength.
    4. courage.
    5. an openness to change.

11. In the program <u>Jazz/Bach</u>, visuals included a sequence that showed a brook, then a river, then the ocean. This sequence was repeated several times. What point was it making?

    1. Humanity will at last free itself from bondage.
    2. Freedom is achieved within the bounds of a discipline.
    3. The ecological cycle of nature has been disrupted.
    4. The art of music emerged from unlikely beginnings.
    5. The obscure artist will, if he or she has integrity, finally gain recognition.

12. It is said that great minds often run in similar channels. One of the following could conceivably have created the final act of King Lear had not its author done so.

    1. Shakespeare
    2. Euripides
    3. Aristotle
    4. Chaplin
    5. Miller

13. A person who attended many performances of both tragic and comic drama would very probably be

    1. clear-thinking.
    2. hyperstimulated.
    3. cynical.
    4. optimistic.
    5. spiritual.

14. In the same way a piece of sculpture depends upon the empty space surrounding it, the basic elements in music are made possible by

    1. tonality.
    2. rhythm.
    3. melody.
    4. silence.
    5. harmony.

15. According to the program <u>Sound to Music</u>, the average listener's idea of melody is derived from which of the following styles of music?

    1. Eastern
    2. contemporary concert music
    3. polyphonic music
    4. romantic music
    5. harmony

16. A spontaneous variation or set of variations on a standard musical theme is called

    1. counter melodic
    2. stylization

56

3. recapitulation
4. improvisation
5. dissonance

17. <u>Jazz/Bach</u> is not only the title of one of the programs you saw, but a word coinage in that program. Which of the following BEST approximates its meaning?

1. collaboration
2. music's transcendence of time and racial barriers
3. the age-old conflict between the classical and the popular music
4. the rebellious spirit of humanity
5. none of the above

18. Directors like Hitchcock, Bergman, and Woody Allen are designated <u>auteurs</u> because

1. they have managed to combine financial and artistic success in their films.
2. they use existential themes.
3. they all write their own scripts.
4. their work can be analyzed as if it were literature.
5. they make daring experiments that make them box-office risks.

19. The peculiar form of comic irony employed by Swift in "A Modest Proposal" is based on which of the following?

1. the reader's previous knowledge of the subject
2. the apparent harmlessness of the subject
3. the narrator's apparent endorsement of the subject
4. the "nonsense" language, which turns out to have meaning
5. a complete lack of any reference to reality

20. Which of the following is identified as a rogue hero?

1. Charlie Chaplin
2. Lucy Arnaz
3. Orgon
4. Tom Jones
5. Hawkeye Pierce

21. To the jazz musician, freedom never just happens; it

1. is a consequence of discipline and mastery of form.
2. comes after a hard fought battle against social prejudice.
3. has to be carefully written into the score.
4. arises from a proficiency in more than one instrument.
5. requires that the musician maintain an open attitude to all types of music.

22. The hero of the oldest work of literature known (which also happens to be a tragedy) is which of the following?

1. Gulliver
2. Macbeth
3. Hamlet

4. Gilgamesh
5. Shamash

23. Which playwright objected to the traditional belief that tragic heroes needed to be persons of high rank and created a modern tragedy about an ordinary man?

    1. Arthur Miller
    2. Charlie Chaplin
    3. James Joyce
    4. Neil Simon
    5. Henri Bergson

24. One of the major reasons for the revival of folk music in the 1960s was that young people saw it as a means of

    1. warding off feelings of alienation and fragmentation.
    2. rejecting their cultural heritage.
    3. rediscovering their lost religious faith.
    4. rediscovering earlier non-sexist attitudes.
    5. I don't know.

25. Enjoying one particular kind of music all the time is to

    1. know only one side of one's personality.
    2. demonstrate that one has developed a fine critical discernment.
    3. emulate Woodrow Tatlock.
    4. keep many emotions unexplored.
    5. do 1, 3, and 4 above.

26. Aristotle said of tragedy that its purpose was "through pity and terror" to bring about the _____ of those emotions.

    1. intensification
    2. actualization
    3. opposite
    4. reinforcement
    5. purgation

27. Which of the following observations best summarizes an attitude expressed in the chapter "Two Masks"?

    1. Frivolous moments are also part of being human.
    2. Tragedy appeals to people whose killer instinct is never satisfied.
    3. The greatest comedies are concerned with the tragic flaw in comic characters.
    4. A sense of the tragic is more appropriate for human beings than a sense of the comic.
    5. A sense of humor is basic to the rational and moral foundation of human society.

28. In your opinion, which of the following newspaper headlines would Euripides probably find most interesting as a possible subject for a play?

    1. CONVICTED MURDERER PAYS ULTIMATE PENALTY FOR CRIME

58

2.   FERRY SINKS; HUNDREDS FEARED LOST
3.   CONVICTED MURDERER DIES IN GAS CHAMBER MINUTES BEFORE STAY OF EXECUTION
4.   CONVICTED MURDERER PARDONED FIVE MINUTES BEFORE TIME OF EXECUTION
5.   GALLANT POLICEMAN SURVIVES NEAR FATAL SHOOTING

29. Sam Hirsch singles out one of the following as probably the greatest humorist of this century.

     1.   W. C. Fields
     2.   Mark Twain
     3.   Joan Rivers
     4.   Charlie Chaplin
     5.   Jonathan Swift

30. Which one of the following reasons accounts for the disappearance of screwball comedy?

     1.   It was not welcome in a country weary of the Depression.
     2.   People were too concerned about the approaching war to want to see comedy.
     3.   Since the thirties, movies have downgraded women, who had significant roles in screwball comedies.
     4.   Spectacular visual effects have replaced people's interest in witty dialog.
     5.   Screwball comedy is not financially rewarding enough for recent producers.

31. The artistic quality of Citizen Kane came about

     1.   in spite of its being designed as a purely commercial enterprise.
     2.   as a result of Orson Welles' artistic genius and integrity.
     3.   as a result of the powerful persona of the central character.
     4.   because of the American audience's distrust of material success.
     5.   because of the remarkable teamwork of the cast.

32. The theory entitled "The Persistence of Vision with Regard to Moving Objects" explains why

     1.   our vision is not interrupted when we blink.
     2.   early films seem jerky in motion.
     3.   a negative after-image appears when we blink after looking into strong sunlight.
     4.   we think the actors are actually moving in the film.
     5.   1 and 4.

33. All of the following are elements of a symphony EXCEPT one. Which is it?

     1.   recapitulation
     2.   exposition
     3.   monochords
     4.   development
     5.   melody

34. It is suggested in the text that the importance we in the West place on theme in music is related to

     1.   our materialistic nature.

59

2.   the difficulty of understanding music without it.
3.   the unfamiliarity of Eastern sounds.
4.   the requirements of counterpoint.
5.   a stress on individualism.

35. Edwin S. Porter is said to have revolutionized film making in

    1.   the lingering take.
    2.   the elongated moment.
    3.   musical background.
    4.   the cut.
    5.   the actor as persona.

36. D. W. Griffith in <u>The Birth of a Nation</u> was the first motion picture director to

    1.   use innovative techniques.
    2.   show definite directing style.
    3.   use a plot.
    4.   manipulate audience emotion by camera angle.
    5.   use simultaneous action scenes.

37. The jerky movements of the characters in Mack Sennett comedies are the result of

    1.   inferior cameras that couldn't record at high speed.
    2.   the deliberate manipulation of camera and projector speed for comic effects.
    3.   the shortage of experienced camera men because of the war.
    4.   the fact that the audience was satisfied with "primitive" movie art as long as there was action.
    5.   an attempt on the director's part to reflect the widespread neurosis of the times.

38. Chapter 4 of the text makes the point that Eisenstein in directing <u>Potemkin</u>

    1.   uses the film medium first and foremost as a vehicle for propaganda.
    2.   presents powerful propaganda but transcends it artistically.
    3.   presents a plea for reconciliation of Royalists and Soviet citizens.
    4.   displeased Soviet critics with his innovations.
    5.   introduced the use of montage in motion pictures.

39. The best films of the silent era were those which

    1.   were totally visual, using only images to communicate.
    2.   used word cards so that audiences understood what the actors were saying.
    3.   found ways to communicate linguistic subtleties.
    4.   had tragic endings, despite audience preferences for optimistic ones.
    5.   had the biggest budget to work with and could therefore use location sites outside Hollywood.

40. The film version of Thomas Hardy's <u>Tess of the D'Urbervilles</u> is presented in the text as an example of

    1.   a producer's losing money but maintaining artistic integrity

2. Hollywood's betrayal of artistic integrity to uphold popular moral attitudes.
3. the producer and director's cinematically affirming the author's pessimistic view of life.
4. a film version of a novel that, for once, made the author happy.
5. a virtually unknown actor's rise to fame in a single movie.

41. Screwball comedy was a popular genre of the 1930s that was characterized by

1. serio-comic commentary on the Great Depression.
2. violent, dehumanizing action.
3. pathetic underdogs.
4. plotless encounters.
5. short scenes, witty dialog.

42. In Citizen Kane, Orson Welles made theatrical use of

1. deep shadows and underlighted scenes.
2. exploiting the persona of the central character.
3. alternating scenes in black and white with scenes in color.
4. Shakespearean poetic rhythms underlying the prose dialog.
5. unstructured, stream-of-consciousness story line.

43. Citizen Kane is particularly effective screen art because

1. the dialog is colorful and witty.
2. the camera functions cinematically as the central character's point of view.
3. the happy ending is consistent with the optimistic theme of the movie.
4. the acting style was revolutionary for its time.
5. it introduced the sophisticated use of the lingering take.

44. The screen art achieved in Casablanca is attributed in large part to

1. the acting of the whole cast.
2. the powerful anti-Nazi theme.
3. the fast pace of the action.
4. the witty dialog.
5. the persona of the main character.

MODULE V

Philosophy: The Question of Reality

OVERVIEW

Philosophers are people who spend a great deal of time thinking about matters that many of us consider unimportant or at least without immediate relevance to the practical affairs of everyday life. They even tackle questions, such as whether or not God exists, which they know in advance may not yield final answers. Why are there such people, and what do they mean--or perhaps should they mean to us?

Whether or not such a thing as "truth" exists as an absolute, unchanging entity, still a certain rare few in every era are convinced that they can make a case for what they believe to be true. They persist, even though they anticipate--and indeed expect--someone else to challenge their thought. Thinking for the sake of thinking--thinking for other than immediately practical reasons--can set us apart from other creatures. Some thinkers, such as Socrates himself, the father of philosophy, have even given up their lives for the right to question what others say is true and to teach others how to think for themselves. For once one develops the habit of pursuing truth, it is difficult to be satisfied with a lesser use of the mind.

Oftentimes philosophers, in seeking to understand and interpret the world, come upon a vision of things as they might be rather than as they are; and the core of their work is description, perhaps of an ideal society, or of the perfect way for a human being to live. They are the idealists among us, and even though we might question the value of describing what will never be, they do provide us with the means of evaluating the world around us and wondering what we might do to make it better.

But philosophy need not supply us with a utopian vision. Indeed we cannot say in advance what philosophy ought to be or what in each instance it will turn out to be. Philosophers' mental journeys take them where their ideas lead, even if the end result is a question mark. Their value lies not necessarily in the final destination but in illustrating for us the process of careful, sustained thought. If we give ourselves the chance to engage in such an activity, we shall experience what human consciousness can be like at a very high and exhilarating level.

LEARNING OBJECTIVES

Having completed this module, you should be able to

1) cite a variety of interpretations of "certainty" and ways of achieving it, according to philosophers, theologians, and scientists.

63

2)   cite philosophers who have invoked logic rather than science alone to prove God's existence.

3)   demonstrate an awareness of difficulties which have historically existed for those who have elected faith over science (e.g., the problem of evil).

4)   indicate when and why the scientific method, as we now know it, began to emerge in human culture.

5)   point out significant events in the long conflict between faith and science.

6)   point out contemporary trends that indicate that the conflict is far from resolved.

7)   explain as simply as possible theories in modern physics dealing with origins of the universe, especially those of the Big Bang, black holes, and single force.

8)   identify human needs which create utopian idealism.

9)   present your own views regarding the practicality and desirability of conscious utopian experiments.

10)   contrast the approaches to living embodied in the characters of Don Quixote and Sancho Panza.

11)   compare attitudes toward free choice in the ideal societies of Plato, More, Thoreau, and Skinner.

AS YOU READ

Chapter 5: "The Philosophers"

1. The chapter presents the approaches of philosophers through the ages to three large concepts: the idea of mind, the idea of God, and the idea of reality. Be able to state how the philosophers cited in this chapter have responded to these ideas.

2. Show how the classical concept of _mind_ leads to acceptance of the idea of life after death.

3. What definition of _mind_ does Plato's theory of the Forms give us?

4. If we do not know the Forms, that is, abstractions such as justice, beauty, etc., through the experience of our senses whence, according to Plato, does our knowledge of them come?

5. What would Plato say to the belief that values like right and wrong are relative to time, place, and culture?

6. The contemporary philosopher Mortimer J. Adler agrees with certain elements of Plato's philosophy. Identify them and then be able to show what aspects of Plato's thinking he would revise.

7. Be familiar with Descartes' method of achieving certainty and the philosophical criticisms of his method.

8. Plato and his pupil Aristotle disagreed profoundly on at least one major point. What was it? What position did each one take?

9. Shortly after the advent of Christianity, the philosophy of Stoicism had its greatest impact on Roman thought. What was the underlying premise?

10. Summarize some of the major problems which early Christian beliefs posed for rationalism.

11. How does St. Augustine account for the existence of evil in the world? Did he believe that humanity could comprehend God?

12. Summarize St. Anselm's ontological argument for God's existence.

13. Make certain you are familiar with the basic premises of St. Thomas Aquinas's five arguments for God's existence.

14. The American philosopher Charles Sander Peirce denies the existence of God. What are his arguments? What objections to his arguments have been raised?

15. What were the basic concerns of the early Greek philosophers and scientists, known as the Pre-Socratics?

16. Who first suggested an atomic theory? Can you mention at least one way in which the theory has since been modified?

17. Be able to discuss a major impact Charles Darwin had upon religion.

18. What were Kant's and James's positions on the provability of God's existence?

19. Be familiar with the explanations given in the Big Bang theory about the beginnings of the physical universe. How does this theory involve both scientific and philosophical inquiry?

20. Point out similar elements in Aquinas's ontological argument and some theories of modern particle physicists. Do the latter give answers to questions about the nature and origin of the "First Substance"?

VIEWING

I. The Outer Circle

   --To make sense of your own life, it is necessary to recognize your own world

65

view. Three main world views appear in the conflicts described in The Outer Circle: faith versus reason; reason versus science; and objective science versus inner truth.

--The opening scene takes place in a medieval European town. The singer is one of the Goliards, wandering university scholars who composed and sang Latin songs - lyrics, drinking songs, and satires on contemporary society. This young man, then, represents a questioning attitude toward the limitations imposed upon thought and experience by traditional authority.

--When one of the Goliards, in challenging the dogma being presented to the class, asks the teacher how "human reason knows enough to accept such matters," he is summing up the dissatisfaction with faith that had been building for several centuries. From within the ranks of Christianity itself were to come young minds who would insist upon the attainment of religious certainty through logical methods that would satisfy, not evade, the demands of reason. This sweeping philosophical movement was called Scholasticism.

--The troubled Goliard is seen in his cell, asking himself questions that typify the struggle between faith and reason. He finds himself scraping his head against the "outer circle" of his particular age: that is, the positive limits of human thought, beyond which it is not permitted for him to go in his speculations.

--He recalls that Saint Augustine, about 600 years before, had peered beyond his own outer circle, asking such questions as these: "How could God have used a voice to order the various stages of creation, if He were pure spirit and if, before there was a creation, nothing physical existed?" and "What materials did God use to make the earth when no materials could have been there at all?" and "Where did God make the earth if no place existed?" Augustine's answer had been that reason cannot grasp such paradoxes, but faith has no trouble doing so. Faith has even been defined as the capacity for accepting paradoxes.

--The next cell we see is that belonging to Galileo, a 17th century scientist and astronomer, who developed the telescope and sextant and thus was able to assert some things--such as his confirmation of the Copernican heliocentric theory of the universe--that were not exactly popular with the Church. In the case of Galileo, it was science that broke through the outer circle, setting off a series of fierce confrontations with faith.

--The universe of Isaac Newton was in a sense the scientific counterpart of the Church's universe that it would supplant in many minds. It was a fixed and finite system, but governed by purely physical laws, all of which science would supposedly discover. The Newtonian world view inspired a new kind of religion, deism, which maintained that God had designed and created this beautifully rational, well run world machine and then had turned His thoughts to other matters, leaving the world to operate strictly in accordance with natural law, with never any divine intervention.

--Darwin's theory of evolution (1859) set off an even more intense confrontation between faith and science than had Galileo's support for the Copernican world view, one that saw many different interpretations emerging. The "moderate" position was that perhaps God had wanted to create man in an evolutionary manner, but here the crucial question centered on the nature and source of the human mind. Had it evolved? Or had it been bestowed by God? If so, why just this one exception in an otherwise natural process?

--Pierre Teilhard de Chardin was both a physicist and a Jesuit priest, developing a theory of evolution that synthesized his religious faith and scientific knowledge. Teilhard believed that evolution was both physical and spiritual, that Jesus represented an extraordinarily early embodiment of the spiritual and moral perfection toward which humankind was aspiring, and that one day Jesus would reemerge, this time as the Super Christ, taking his destined place of leadership among a developed race now prepared to understand and live by his philosophy. Do you see the importance of recognizing one's own world view?

--As you are watching people on an escalator going past an airline security guard, a reference is made to Aldous Huxley's novel, Brave New World. This is a fable about a world state in the 7th century A.F. (After Ford), when every human activity is scientifically regulated in the interest of a trouble-free society.

--The Goliard returns, this time in modern dress, and finds himself facing a new outer circle, a new set of limitations. Once more he challenges the circle. Note that the program itself has come full circle, ending as it began with a conflict. Will it always be this way? Do you think it should be?

II. The Pursuit of the Ideal

--Speculative philosophers think about matters most people don't concern themselves about. One fundamental question inevitably is what represents the ideal--from the individual struggling to win a rodeo, live alone in the woods, or make a perfect ceramic to the utopian with a grandiose scheme for ordering the activities of everyone in the world.

--The first part of Don Quixote was published in 1605. In it Cervantes depicts an aging scholar whose mind has been addled by reading the sentimental romances of chivalry so popular in Spain at the time. He sees himself as a knight pursuing lofty ideas and combating evil. Sancho Panza, his "squire," is just the opposite. Unhampered by an imagination run wild, he sees actual windmills, not ferocious giants. Sancho Panza deals with things as they come and settles for necessary compromises in an imperfect world.

--In the second part of the novel, published in 1615 after Cervantes' death, Don Quixote appears in a different light. He is no longer so ridiculous as a man of integrity in an idealized world that operates by more honorable rules of conduct than the real world does. Little by little, Sancho Panza is caught up in the glorious vision. At the end, Don Quixote on his death bed renounces his absurd self-deception and returns to "sanity"; Sancho Panza begs him not to die but to put on his costume and continue the noble adventure. Between them Don Quixote and Sancho Panza pose the central issue of the work: should one pursue an ideal that is forever out of reach but that somehow ennobles the pursuer...or should one admit to the limitations and imperfections of life and make compromises?

--Sir Thomas More's Utopia, published in Latin in 1516, is a traveler's tale narrated by a philosopher-mariner. The first part criticizes the abuse of power and wealth in England during the time of Henry VIII. The second part describes the ideal commonwealth of Utopia, where all the citizens are happy because they have been taught as children to despise money and thus have abolished greed.

--Socrates, who is Plato's spokesman in The Republic, diagnosed the moral decline of Athens after the war with Sparta and formulated a plan for an ideal state that would restore a natural order. The Republic was to be an aristocracy, not in a political but in an ethical sense. The population would be divided into classes according to their abilities, and the classes would be carefully constructed; marriages would be arranged on principles of genetics; children would be assigned, for rearing, to the most appropriate adults. The classes-- rulers (or guardians), soldiers, and workers--were permanently fixed. The guardians of the state would be chosen from those who exhibited the highest intellectual and moral attainment. The most eminent intellectually would be the kings.

--B. F. Skinner developed his theory of "operant conditioning" by observing that pigeons and rats in the laboratory could be trained by reinforcements to behave in an expected way where there was an apparent possibility of alternate choices. Skinner believes that human behavior can likewise be conditioned--and should be, for the good of society. He defends what some consider a violation of human freedom on the grounds that everybody is conditioned anyhow--by climate, education, government for instance. But under the illusion that they are able-- and entitled--to make free choices in their personal interest, people have brought civilization to the brink of disaster. In Sir Thomas More's Utopia, which is envisioned on more traditionally humanistic values than Skinner's proposal, the people are nevertheless deliberately conditioned in childhood to despise the things that work against the communal good.

--Thoreau believed that the ideal would lie in having the freedom to live as one wishes. In his book Walden, he depicted the pleasure of a simple solitary existence lived in close harmony with nature. But Thoreau was also intensely concerned with social issues. He distrusted all institutions, asserting that government ought to "govern not at all." His essay "Civil Disobedience" became a kind of master-plan for social reform through nonviolent resistance. On one occasion Thoreau even went to jail rather than pay what he regarded as an unfair tax.

SELF-TEST

Match each item in the first column with an item in the second. Use no item more than once.

T 1.	knowledge for Plato	conflict between predestination and free will resolved by faith alone	_____
T 2.	St. Thomas Aquinas		
T 3.	Democritus	created symbol of impractical idealist	_____
T 4.	God known "practically not rationally"	theory of operant conditioning	_____
V 5.	outer circle	achieved certainty through doubting	_____
T 6.	nothing greater than God can be conceived	with us from birth	_____
V 7.	Cervantes	argues against the existence of God	_____
V 8.	B. F. Skinner		
V 9.	Teilhard du Chardin	classical model of utopian ideas	_____
V 10.	The Republic	spiritual evolution	_____
T 11.	Rene Descartes	developed first atomic theory	_____
T 12	St. Augustine	five proofs of God's existence	_____
T 13.	Charles Sander Peirce	St. Anselm's ontological argument	_____
		Kant	_____
		limits human imagination and insight	_____

CHECK LIST OF MAIN IDEAS

1. Historically, human beings have been obsessed with questions of how the world originated, how reality is known, and whether human existence has purpose or meaning.

2. Since medieval times, theologians have attempted, with varying degrees of success, to use logic to prove the existence of God, to explain the presence of evil, and to give meaning to human existence.

3. As civilization and science developed, plausible explanations were found for many previously unexplained phenomena, yet many questions remain unanswered.

4. Over the years philosophers have used varying strategies to resolve the question of whether an "ultimate" exists.

> Augustine: Only God could have created the world since nothing can come from nothing without Divine intervention.

> Anselm: Nothing greater than God can be conceived. If God were merely a figment of our imagination, we would be able to conceive of something greater. Hence, God necessarily exists.

> Aquinas: God is the uncaused cause, and the necessary Being from which other beings derive. Since there is design in this world there must be a Designer.

> DesCartes: God is a perfect being; a perfect being must have existence, therefore God exists.

> Kant: We cannot prove God's existence by reason alone, but "practical" philosophy, which is grounded in psychological need, can be just as valid as reason.

> William James: If we wait for proof positive before we do anything, we would be immobile. Belief is desirable when it makes a positive contribution to the individual's psyche.

> Teilhard de Chardin: Humanity is evolving toward the Omega Point, where it will have achieved nobility, genius, and the capacity for love. Christ was the model for this form of human nature.

Existentialists: We must accept that the world is absurd and go on from there.

5. The Big Bang theory is the explanation of the origins of the universe most widely accepted by modern physicists. It does not, however, address the question of what ultimate reality is, if indeed such a thing exists.

6. There have been a number of philosophers, in quest of answers to questions they have asked, who inevitably come upon a vision of what ought to be the case rather than what is. A good example in very recent times is the possibility that the universe does exhibit a fundamental order--an interpretation of recent scientific thought that some say is unjustified.

7. In this module we have explored several schemes which have been proposed to achieve a perfect society:

   Plato designed a "Republic" in which leaders selected for their intelligence and morality would arrange people's lives.

   Sir Thomas More proposed a "Utopia" wherein all property is held in common and education and religious freedom are available to all.

   B. F. Skinner suggested a "Walden II" in which people are conditioned (by positive and negative reinforcement) so as to behave in a manner that works for their own and society's good.

8. We have a choice to make: we can risk the consequences of freely pursuing our individual goals or we can submit ourselves to the dictates of a society that would impose its definition of the good life on us.

9. In general, the humanist would opt for cautious commitment to ideals and freedom of individual action to the degree that it does not infringe upon the free choice of others.

A CONFLICT FOR ALL SEASONS

by

Joan Cronin

In Western culture a faith/reason dualism appears to have emerged for the first time in the 5th century when St. Augustine attempted to reconcile the fact of evil in the world with Christian belief in a benevolent God. It is a question that has since preoccupied most of the major religions of the world. Briefly stated: we observe that pain, death, earthquake, injustice, and cruelty do exist in the world. If God were all-good, He would not <u>will</u> these to be; if He were all powerful, He would not <u>allow</u> them to be. Augustine offered a solution in rational terms: evil does not have actual existence; it is the absence of good, but man is free to choose the good. Therefore, the responsibility for evil in the world is man's, not God's.

But part of the problem of evil could not be solved by rational analysis. Augustine taught that God preordained certain individuals to repent and be saved, and others to suffer their just punishment. But a troubling question arises: how can man choose freely if his choice is predestined? Augustine's answer was that the mystery of grace and redemption as revealed in the Holy Scripture is a matter of faith and cannot be rationally understood. The limitation this placed on reason has powerfully influenced religious thought down to our own century; but the enigmas of evil and the suffering of the innocent continue to challenge both faith and reason.

While faith continued for centuries to be an essential source of truth in Christian thought, events in the secular world could not but introduce change in the religious experience. In the 8th century, western Europe was united under Charlemagne in a single Christian empire. Until this time, monasteries had been the only centers of learning, and their purpose had been limited to educating the clergy. In 787 Charlemagne ordered the establishment of schools in connection with every abbey in the realm. Great scholars came together at these schools, and learning took on a far more speculative nature than would have been congenial in the monasteries. An interest in logic and rational values grew up side by side with, but independent of, a reliance on revelation. The minds of Christians became increasingly critical. Attempts to see the universe as intelligible were accompanied by an insistence that God too must be intelligible by reason as well as by faith.

The term "Scholasticism" is given to the intellectual movement begun in these abbey schools. The unique characteristic of scholastic thought is that it was able to harmonize faith and reason as compatible sources of knowledge, resting on one absolute truth that transcended both. The scholastic thinkers, by pushing back the limits formerly set on reason, were responsible for the rebirth of philosophy, which

72

had disappeared from European thought since the closing of the philosophical schools of Athens in 529.

In the 13th century, St. Thomas Aquinas represented a synthesis of theology and philosophy that unified medieval thought on every subject of inquiry, natural for supernatural. Aquinas taught that there are mysteries--like the nature of God--that cannot be understood by reason; they are made manifest only by divine revelation and apprehended only by faith. However, he believed that the existence of God could be demonstrated by logical inference from the operation of the natural world.

It was also believed that, if the human mind could comprehend God's existence, it could easily comprehend the natural world as well. For Aquinas, reason could not help affirming the existence of a marvelously designed natural universe, one that the Greek astronomer Ptolemy had incorrectly viewed as geocentric.

The earth had been created by God at the very center of the universe, as a fitting home for man, whom He had made in His own image and likeness. Man's whole dignity lay in his crucial position: only one degree below God's angels. The geocentric system of astronomy also provided a model for all the hierarchies of medieval society. The church, society, the natural world were seen as systems in which authority descended from God in fixed and strictly ordered degrees. Thus did reason and faith appear to join forces--to explain both worlds.

Yet out of the synthesis emerged the scientific movement, almost inevitably. Curiosity over the workings of the beautiful design proved irresistible. In 1473 a Polish astronomer named Nicholas Copernicus was born. He was to formulate the theory that the sun was at the center of the universe, with earth merely one of the planets revolving around it. Later, in the 17th centruy Galileo was able to demonstrate the theory with more of science's technology at hand.

Galileo developed a telescope powerful enough to permit observation of the satellites revolving around the planet Jupiter. He recognized in this phenomenon a miniature system that substantiated the Copernican heliocentric theory.

Galileo was forbidden by Pope Paul V to teach or to defend his discovery, but in 1623 he published it in his "Dialogue on the Two Greatest Systems of the Universe," which compared the Ptolemaic and Copernican theories. Galileo was summoned before the Inquisition and condemned as "vehemently suspected of heresy." Under a probable fear of torture he recanted his statements but was sentenced to involuntary confinement to his home. He gradually went blind, but even so, he continued his scientific activity as long as he could.

Galileo's great contribution to the scientific movement was the application of mathematical formulas to a direct observation of nature. He was the first to interpret the heavens as a mechanical system, preparing the way for the Newtonian world view that dominated the 17th and 18th centuries.

Synthesizing the discoveries made from the time of Copernicus to his own age, Newton described an intelligible and orderly physical universe, working with predictable perfection, the so-called "World Machine." He discovered the laws of gravitation, light and motion, but viewed the order in the universe as an indication of the existence of God.

Newton did not believe that his description of the universe was complete, but it was accepted in the following century as a total theory of nature and the God of nature. Eighteenth century deism was a scientifically oriented religion that held God to be a detached, impersonal power which had created the world, given it physical laws that it might govern itself with perfect regularity, and then withdrawn--never again to interfere with its workings. The most significant aspect of 18th century philosophy was that these laws of nature were discovered not through revelation but this time by the exclusive exercise of human reason.

By the 19th century the discoveries in astronomy, geology, archaeology, and biology were vigorously reinforcing the sovereignty of reason and science. The tenets of old faiths seemed to collapse as even spiritual truths were tested by the language and methods of science. In opposition to the overwhelming impact of science on religion, an intense revival of faith occurred.

In England the revival manifested itself in the Oxford Movement within the Anglican Church. John Henry Newman was one of the central figures in this movement, which was also called "Tractarianism," from the series of ninety tracts published to express its religious views. Believing that reason could not prevent the onslaught of science on religion, Newman urged a return to the dogmatic authority of the Church fathers, to the Bible as a source of revealed truth, and to the medieval color of religious ritual.

Newman especially urged resistance to the exclusive application of reason to religious teaching. Eventually this position was rejected as too conservative for others in the Anglican Church, and Newman believed that the Anglican Church was too liberal for him to find religious certainty in it. He entered the Roman Catholic priesthood and in 1879 became a Cardinal.

Newman's contemporary, Thomas Henry Huxley, on the other hand, defended the view that religious truth had to pass the test of scientific thinking. Huxley coined the word "agnostic" to describe his own position: that of one who did not know whether or not God existed. When rational inquiry fails to provide evidence for a belief, Huxley said, the honest course is to suspend judgment rather than to assent on the basis of blind faith. Huxley was a staunch supporter of Charles Darwin in the 19th century's most dramatic conflict between science and faith.

Darwin's theory of biological evolution, published in On the Origin of Species in 1859, produced an uproar in European society. Darwin advanced the belief that all forms of life, including the human, have developed from more primitive forms; that chance variations made it possible for some forms to survive the struggle for existence; and that these variations were inherited by descendants. This theory was attacked as a sacrilegious contradiction of revealed truth about the dignity of man and his purpose in the world. People were not prepared to see themselves as descendants of brute beasts in a universe governed by blind chance.

Where Newton had been able to reconcile the results of his scientific investigations with the prevalent ethical and religious beliefs of this time, Darwin could not. The conflict reached a climax in 1925 in the trial of John Scopes, a Tennessee school teacher. Scopes was arrested for breaking the state law against teaching the theory of evolution. He was defended by Clarence Darrow, a famous attorney who championed freedom of speech and inquiry. The prosecutor was William Jennings Bryan, a former presidential candidate who held firm religious views on the literal interpretation of the biblical account of creation. Scopes was found guilty and fined, but it was not a defeat for Darwin's theory. Darwin had been honored by many of the learned societies of Europe. His ideas were widely influential among scientific thinkers, and many people had come to see in the concept of evolution a promise of unlimited human and material progress.

Today, however, the situation has almost reversed itself; there is a growing distrust of the autonomy of reason and an upsurge in religious faith. Science, many feel, is propelling us not toward a golden age of humanity but toward a technological nightmare. In the early 19th century the poet William Blake expressed his fear that the visionary imagination would be sacrificed in the "dark Satanic mills" of the Industrial Revolution. To many there is ample cause to fear the sacrifice of human values to scientific abstractions. When science insists that the end justifies the means and at the same time divorces itself from a moral responsibility rooted in faith, some argue, the research on human guinea pigs at Buchenwald is made possible; and the holocausts of Nagasaki and Hiroshima, not to mention the agony of Viet Nam, become "rational" ways of solving human problems.

RECOMMENDED READING

Mortimer J. Adler. Ten Philosophical Mistakes (New York: MacMilliam 1985). The
    author sometimes considered the greatest living philosopher, presents his views
    on basic errors in modern thought and how they can be avoided.

Maxwell Anderson. Barefoot in Athens (New York: Dramatists Play Service, 1952). A
    highly entertaining account of the life of Socrates, containing debates about
    the usefulness of a life devoted to rational thought.

Crane Brinton. Ideas and Men: The Story of Western Thought (Englewood Cliffs,
    N.J.: Prentice-Hall, 1963).

Nigel Calder. Einstein's Universe (New York: Viking Press, 1979; Penguin 1980).
    An easy-to-read summary of the special and general theories of relatively, upon
    which much contemporary thought is based.

Miguel Cervantes. Don Quixote (Appears in various editions and translations). The
    famous picaresque novel about a mad idealist's search for perfection.

Robert P. Crease and Charles C. Mann. The Second Creation (New York: Macmillan,
    1986). An extraordinary work which goes deeply into the thought processes of
    major contemporary physicists and traces the development of speculative
    scientific thought as it is at this very moment.

Charles Darwin. On the Origin of Species (New York: Modern Library, 1936). The
    classic work delineating the theory of evolution.

_____. Voyage of the Beagle ed. M. E. Selsam (New York, Harper, 1959). A
    fascinating compendium of Darwin's meticulous notes from the expedition of the
    Beagle, the voyage during which he began to formulate his famous biological
    theories.

Zsolt Harsanyi. The Star Gazer tr. Paul Tabor (New York: G. P. Putnam's Sons,
    1939).A beautifully written fictionalized biography of Galileo.

Stephen W. Hawking. A Brief History of Time (New York: Bantam, 1988). A widely
    read physicist of our time shares his speculations on the beginnings of the
    universe and questions whether there were indeed beginnings.

Aldous Huxley. Brave New World (Appears in various editions.) Originally published
    in 1932, this novel of the future is frighteningly prophetic; education has
    become regimented, the humanities have all but disappeared from the scene. The
    government counteracts the potentially dangerous effect of boredom by freely
    dispensing drugs to the citizens.

William James. "The Will to Believe" in The Will to Believe and other essays in
    popular philosophy (New York: Dover, 1956). A short essay delineating the
    differences between beliefs that are possible and those that are not. The
    distinction lies on psychological, not logical grounds.

Herman Melville. Moby Dick (New York: W. W. Norton, 1967). It is in this powerful allegory (hailed by many as the greatest novel in the English language) that Ahab confronts the white whale, which could symbolize either the evil on earth or the moral neutrality of the universe.

Sir Thomas More. <u>Utopia</u> (New York: Yale University Press, 1964). A satire on the inequalities of Henry VIII's England and the delineation of a perfect communal society.

B. F. Skinner. <u>Walden Two</u> (New York: MacMillian, 1971.) A controversial novel of a scientifically-shaped Utopia by a leading behaviorist.

Pierre Teilhard de Chardin. <u>Let Me Explain</u> (New York: Harper and Row, 1970). An informal presentation of the author's beliefs on the evolution of human spirituality.

Philosophy: Moral Values

OVERVIEW

Any number of conflicting moral values seem to underlie human actions. The blood of millions has been shed in the name of moral principles. The human race has, for this and many other reasons, always been and continues to be deeply concerned over moral issues. The foundation question in moral philosophy is: <u>where do moral values come from</u>? Answers are readily available, but, once we have some within our grasp, we are led to a thornier set of problems, such as the basis for choosing among possible moral sources. In one corner sit reason, religion, and a host of universal "shoulds"; in the other, the principle that morality can relate only to specific situations, that in the final analysis all sides of moral issues need to be considered. One profound, noteworthy--and in the opinion of some, tragically insufficient--attempt to solve the dilemma in terms of today's society is existentialism, a philosophy that stresses freedom of moral choice but makes the individual solely responsible for the consequences.

LEARNING OBJECTIVES

Having completed this module, you should be able to

1) summarize the basic concerns in moral philosophy.

2) define moral values and moral sanctions in rational, religious, cultural, familial, and personal terms.

3) distinguish among popular slogans, the public moral conscience, and work as factors in moral philosophy.

4) explain and distinguish among the moral viewpoints taken by Socrates, Marx, Sartre, and the situationalists.

5) summarize the parable of Gyges and its applications to moral philosophy.

6) relate the parable of Abraham and Isaac to fundamental issues in moral philosophy.

7) compare the roles of authority and freedom in existential moral philosophy.

Chapter 6: "The Moral Issue"

1. Why is the whole issue of morality somewhat cloudy? Why is there so much confusion over what constitutes moral action?

2. What is the Ring of Gyges? Be able to define in your own words what it represents in philosophy.

3. Socrates maintained that the rational person will act justly whether or not his actions are known. What is the principle Socratic argument in defense of this assertion?

4. The Utilitarians share with Aristotle the belief that the state exists to promote the good life of the citizen. In what important respect do the theories differ?

5. How did Glaucon disagree with Socrates? With whom do you agree?

6. The chapter calls the debate between reason and self-interest an historical one. In a few choice sentences, explain the debate.

7. What sides do Kant and Bentham take in the debate referred to above?

8. Mill stated that the public moral conscience can be tyrannical. How is it used to suppress justice or new ideas?

9. Why is "of course" such an important barometer of our moral values?

10. Find two or three slogans in the chapter which have influenced your own moral philosophy. Or two or three that are not mentioned.

11. Describe some ways in which having a job influences moral values.

12. Be able to analyze the three major components in a given moral issue.

13. Do you believe that moral choice depends upon the situation? Cite examples which defend this position. Can you think of any which could be used to argue against it?

14. What was existentialism as Kierkegaard defined it? What additions were made by Sartre? In Sartre's philosophy, how does believing that life is absurd affect behavior?

15. Is moral integrity worthwhile when it is not repaid in kind? Think of people you have known who seem to exemplify moral integrity, and those who do not. Which appear to be the most successful? Most content?

16. What historical evidence is there to support or refute the theory that the free market is "self-correcting"? What has this issue to do with morality?

I. The Ring of Gyges

--The title refers to a parable related by a character named Glaucon in one of the
  dialogs in Plato's Republic. In order to disprove Socrates' argument that
  anyone who knows the right thing will do it because virtue is synonymous with
  reason, Glaucon tells the story of the shepherd, Gyges. Gyges found a ring that
  gave him the power to disappear at will. Gyges used this power to steal, rape,
  and murder. Because his actions were not seen, his reputation did not suffer,
  and he was not punished. Glaucon concluded that all people would act as Gyges
  did if it were not for fear that they would be punished and lose their good name

--The opening sequence involving the narrator and the apparently blind nurseryman
  puts the parable of Gyges into the context of everyday moral dilemmas. In such
  a context we can easily see how often each of us has an opportunity to behave as
  if invisible. The question facing the narrator is precisely the same as that
  posed to Socrates by Glaucon: would I be moral if no one were looking at me?
  Socrates, of course, insists that the man of reason behaves morally whether
  anyone is looking or not. But note that the narrator has problems. Is the
  nurseryman really blind, for example? And what if the cost differential
  amounted to several thousands? No ultimate solution to these questions is given
  in the program, but a number of possibilities are explored.

--The difficulty inherent in the Socratic position, as the narrator soon
  discovers, is that there always appear to be alternate explanations for
  following moral absolutes. For example, should he cheat while invisible? No,
  he will not. Besides, someone might see the pencil writing by itself. Over and
  over we find ourselves confronting the argument of Glaucon, namely, that people
  behave morally to preserve their good name in the eyes of others, not for the
  sake of moral behavior itself.

--Father Walk speaks from the Judeo-Christian moral tradition. His contention is
  that the knowledge of moral good is inborn, placed within us by God, but that,
  because each of us is given freedom of the will, the means of achieving moral
  perfection are left up to the individual. The individual, however, is
  responsible for the sins he commits. In other words, we are free to do as we
  like, but, since we know the difference between right and wrong, we are expected
  to choose the right. Many philosophers have found the Judeo-Christian moral
  philosophy paradoxical.

--Dr. Haber speaks from the viewpoint of behavioral philosophy, which maintains
  that absolute right and absolute wrong do not exist. "Right" is what one's
  society (or peer group or teachers or family) rewards, and "wrong" is what it
  punishes. Difficulties arise from the fact that we become conditioned by a
  number of sources, imposing conflicting values. (The foremost spokesperson for
  behavioral psychology is B. F. Skinner, whose novel Walden Two presents the
  blueprint for a future society conditioned to ethical behavior by scientific
  authorities on behavior.)

II. The Anguish of Abraham

--The title of the program is a phrase made famous by Kierkegaard, the Danish philosopher and founder of existentialism. Kierkegaard used the biblical story of Abraham, the venerable Hebrew patriarch commanded by God to slay his son in sacrifice, as a metaphor of the human predicament. Being mortal, Abraham cannot comprehend God's ways or even be sure that God exists at all. All Abraham can do is act out of his own deep conviction and faith in God, but, says Kierkegaard, he cannot be certain beforehand that the act of sacrifice is right and good. Nonetheless, Abraham must choose whether to commit that sacrifice, guided only by his belief. To Kierkegaard, Abraham in this terrible plight represented humanity caught in the tragic dilemma of having to make fearful choices.

--Kierkegaard also believed, however, that Abraham, in his decision to perform the sacrifice, represented the truly authentic human being: honest, sincere, willing to act, and willing to take responsibility for the outcome. For, had the son Isaac died, Abraham would have had no choice except to bear the guilt for the boy's death. He could not have blamed God, since the commitment was in the name of Abraham's own faith.

--Kierkegaard's conclusion was that nothing is truly certain except the present moment--the existential moment--in which choice confronts us. In committing oneself to action, one takes a "leap of faith" and hopes that all will be well. but in that leap it is impossible to escape the tragic burden of existential anguish.

--The French existentialists, who rediscovered the writings of Kierkegaard in the late 1940s after nearly a century of obscurity, viewed existential anguish, however, as the one condition which gave human life a sense of dignity. For the chooser who acts out of authentic belief and takes responsibility for the consequences of his choice (or refusal to choose, which is also an act of choice), is in fact master of his own destiny. Those who blame others or the times or circumstances for what happens, ignoring their own responsibility, thus avoiding existential anguish, are not full, authentic human beings.

--The story of Edouard, a student at the University of Paris during the flowering of the existential movement, is paralleled with that of Abraham--but with an important switch. The old patriarch must decide whether to kill his son, whereas Edouard must decide whether giving up his life style in Paris will really save his brother's life. Abraham acts out of faith in God and shows his willingness to proceed with the sacrifice (which God, of course, prevents from happening). Edouard delays acting at all and one day finds his brother dead. Edouard achieves his authenticity as a human being by choosing to accept the responsibility for the boy's death over the protests of friends, who insist guilt feelings are not necessary.

--At the end of the program Edouard is seen kneeling by his brother's grave, in the depths of sorrow, but also at the beginning of an authentic life. The young man's attainment of dignity as an authentic human being is symbolized by the change from black and white to color.

--The viewer will also want to consider the symbolism of the brother's kite, which is associated with the idea of freedom. Existentialism is, above all, a philosophy of freedom. Only the authentic person, willing to choose, to bear the burden of anguish, and to take responsibility for his deeds, can consider himself free. Can you see why?

T	1.	Jeremy Bentham	the function of the state is to promote the good life for the citizens	_____
VT	2.	Glaucon		
T	3.	John Stuart Mill	acceptance of guilt	_____
T	4.	emphasis on thoughts as well as deeds	belief that people are selfish and pleasure loving	_____
T	5.	situationalist	theory that government should control big business	_____
VT	6.	Søren Kierkegaard		
			leap of faith	_____
VT	7.	Abraham		
			"Tyranny of the Majority"	_____
V	8.	Edouard's anguish		
			would impose their moral vision on everyone	_____
V	9.	Edouard's decision		
T	10.	Machiavelli	appearance more important than reality	_____
T	11.	laissez faire		
			moral values are universally binding	_____
T	12	Keynesian economics		
T	13.	Immanuel Kant	reluctance to change style	_____
T	14.	Utilitarian party	no universal moral values	_____
T	15.	secular zealots	Adam Smith	_____
			unquestioning faith	_____
			self-interest an acceptable motive for leaders	_____
			Sermon on the Mount	_____

CHECK LIST OF MAIN IDEAS

1. Morals represent the basis of choice among significant options. Problems arise when the alternatives are equal.

2. Through the years humanity has developed varying approaches to morality.

    Plato-Socrates: moral values are based on reason; they are universal and invariable.

    Judeo-Christian tradition: moral laws are handed down by God and must be scrupulously observed.

    Situationalism: the determination of what constitutes moral human behavior should be based upon motive, circumstances, and consequences.

    Christian Existentialism (Kierkegaard): all matters of profound belief represent a choice one makes freely. One obeys God because one has chosen to do so, not because God has commanded obedience.

    Atheistic Existentialism (Sartre): life is absurd and has no meaning or purpose except what we give it. Once we recognize this, we are condemned to determining what we are to be; but we must assume complete responsibility for the being we create.

3. A nagging question remains: Would we be just if it were assured that our misdeeds would remain undiscovered or unpunished?

RECOMMENDED READING

Albert Camus. The Myth of Sisyphus and Other Essays (New York: Modern Library, 1948). A lucid presentation of existential thought by one of its most cogent proponents.

_____. The Plague (New York: Alfred A. Knopf, 1955). A story of the ethical positions an atheistic physician assumes as he battles a fearsome epidemic.

Søren Kierkegaard. Fear and Trembling and Sickness unto Death (Garden City, N. Y.: Doubleday & Co., 1954). The first of these two essays contains the author's famous treatise about Abraham's moral dilemma.

Plato. The Republic tr. Francis MacDonald Cornford (London: Oxford University Press, 1945). Appears in various editions but this translation is recommended. Chapter 5 of Part II is of special interest because it contains "The Ring of Gyges."

Harold H. Watts. The Modern Reader's Guide to the Bible (New York: Harper and Brothers, 1959). Contains scholarship that deals with the Bible as a work of literature evolving over a period of time.

Survey 3

1. The belief that we are born with a mind containing knowledge of universals was
   introduced by

   1. Teilhard du Chardin.
   2. William James.
   3. Democritus.
   4. Descartes.
   5. Plato.

2. Rene Descartes attempted to achieve certainty of God's existence by

   1. using scientific methodology.
   2. a mystical apprehension.
   3. observing order in the physical universe.
   4. applying Scholastic philosophy.
   5. calling on the evidence of his senses.

3. The existence of the force called the Unmoved Mover as first posited by

   1. Democritus.
   2. Anselm.
   3. Aristotle.
   4. Plato.
   5. Augustine.

4. St. Augustine encountered difficulties in reconciling

   1. faith and science.
   2. a good God and the existence of evil.
   3. the Old and New Testament.
   4. free will and divine foreknowledge.
   5. 2 and 4.

5. _____ attempted to prove the existence of God by logical argument:

   1. Immanuel Kant
   2. the Scholastic philosophers
   3. William James

4.   Teilhard du Chardin
5.   Plato

6.   To early philosophers the term <u>substance</u> meant something which

1.   had only material existence.
2.   had only non-material existence.
3.   existed independent of a person's will or awareness.
4.   pre-existed the physical universe.
5.   existed subjectively in a person's mind.

7.   Democritus and Leucippus advanced the theory that the First Substance was

1.   matter.
2.   water.
3.   change.
4.   chaos.
5.   God.

8.   One theory described in Chapter 5 attributes early people's beliefs in the gods to

1.   prescientific explanations of natural phenomena.
2.   an attempt to transcend their fear of death.
3.   misinterpretation of the communication between the right hemisphere of the brain and the left hemisphere.
4.   visitation from extra-terrestrials.
5.   the fact that the divine was more openly manifest at the dawn of human existence.

9.   _____ is cited as the first philosopher to use the concept of <u>God</u> as an intellectual necessity

1.   Democritus
2.   Aristotle
3.   Job
4.   St. Augustine
5.   Mortimer Adler

10. According to one of the following philosophies, freedom is a burden, since a human being is forced to accept responsibility for his choices. This philosophy is

1.   behaviorism.
2.   scientism.
3.   rationalism.
4.   existentialism.
5.   transcendentalism.

11. Both Abraham and the young French student in the film make a momentous existential choice. Abraham's is to go ahead and sacrifice his son if he must. Edouard's is to

1. go ahead and allow his brohter to die.
2. recognize that he and he alone must bear the blame for his brother's death.
3. recognize his brother's death was a biological event for which no one is responsible.
4. sacrifice his own life for his brother.
5. question whether a really merciful God would have allowed an innocent boy to die.

12. In The Anguish of Abraham there is a very definite symbol of human integrity--the kind of authenticity that is gained when a human achieves freedom through the acceptance of responsibility. Which is the symbol?

    1. the kite
    2. the phonograph
    3. the open air cafe
    4. the wine
    5. the window

13. The host/narrator in The Ring of Gyges has a chance to, but does not, steal money from the blind nurseryman or take a higher priced plant. Which of the following states the best reason he refrains from theft?

    1. The nurseryman may not really be blind after all.
    2. He wouldn't steal in full view of the TV audience.
    3. It's easy to be virtuous when the amount is not high.
    4. He knows that stealing, whatever the amount, is wrong.
    5. All of the above are probable reasons.

14. Socrates would agree with all of the following as basic ingredients of moral conduct EXCEPT

    1. universal truths.
    2. self-interest.
    3. absolute justice.
    4. rational awareness.
    5. objectivity.

15. Plato's Republic has as its central subject

    1. education.
    2. art.
    3. love.
    4. justice.
    5. a theory of the beautiful.

16. Which of the following beliefs is Glaucon pointing out by telling the legend of Gyges?

    1. No ethical laws can be formulated which are universally just.
    2. Many persons would act lawlessly if society were not watching.
    3. The ancient ethical concept "might makes right" is correct.
    4. Abraham had little choice concerning the "right" action.
    5. No evil can befall the truly just person.

17. Which of the following elements in the TV program The Ring of Gyges parallels the power of the magic ring in Plato's use of the story?

    1.   the taking of an examination
    2.   the fact that each speaker saw the problem differently
    3.   the blindness of the nurseryman
    4.   the rationality of the narrator
    5.   none of the above

18. In Kierkegaard's use of the story, Abraham's anguish is the result of which of the following factors?

    1.   He doubts that his people are truly God's Chosen Ones.
    2.   Isaac has pleaded that his life be spared.
    3.   Whether he obeys or disobeys God's orders, he will violate a law.
    4.   His faith has already been weakened by past disappointments.
    5.   He can never be certain that his faith is a well-founded one.

19. Sartre says: "Only afterward will he (man) be something, and he himself will have made what he will be." Which of the following is the best explanation of what Sartre means by "afterward"?

    1.   having realized Abraham's anguish
    2.   having realized that man is nothing
    3.   having set in motion the wheels of the just state
    4.   having come to terms with a Categorical Imperative
    5.   having made the necessary leap of faith

20. Utopianism is more than a blueprint for a perfect society. It is a way of life for great numbers of people, who labor incessantly to improve the quality of human life, even if their contributions are small. Which of the following reasons strikes you as being the MOST valid reason for becoming a utopian?

    1.   Idealism enhances one's self-worth whether one's goals are practical or not.
    2.   Happiness is never a static condition; it is always something to work for.
    3.   Principles are important even if reality always seems to work against them.
    4.   It is difficult for a rational person to be happy when he knows many things are wrong and he is doing nothing about them.
    5.   There are no valid reasons. Utopianism is a fool's errand.

21. Hemingway's definition of "moral" would harmonize best with

    1.   situationalism.
    2.   the Hedonic Calculus.
    3.   Socratic absolutes.
    4.   Kierkegaard.
    5.   Kant.

22. In The Republic Glaucon holds that

    1.   religious leaders who preach absolute values are correct.
    2.   rational belief in fixed principles is important.

3. people would stop at nothing if they were sure they wouldn't get caught.
4. individuals will always choose the good.
5. moral integrity is worthwhile even when it goes unrewarded.

23. The words authentic, inauthentic, responsible, and irresponsible are moral terms important in the deliberation of which of the following?

   1. existentialists
   2. absolutists
   3. Marxists
   4. Catholics
   5. Puritans

24. Which film contains a narrator/host who seems to have the ability to appear and to disappear, and who thereby runs into grave moral problems?

   1. The Way of the Humanist
   2. The Ring of Gyges
   3. Jazz/Bach
   4. Divine Discontent
   5. Art: Tell Us Who We Are

25. The man who appears at the beginning and end of The Pursuit of the Ideal has a recurring dream about his own ideal, his own concept of utter perfection. This dream is of

   1. a deserted Pacific island.
   2. a sailboat in a hidden bay.
   3. a cabin nestled in the mountains.
   4. white horses.
   5. all of the above.

26. What was it that initially drove Don Quixote mad?

   1. the decline of chivalry in the world
   2. reading too many chivalric tales
   3. the debasement of women in a feudal society
   4. being hit in the head by a windmill
   5. Sancho Panza'a scornful comments on his idealism

Read carefully the following situation involving a moral choice.

A man discovered that his wife was suffering from a terminal illness and that her remaining days would be very painful. There was, however, a new drug that could alleviate the pain, a drug in very short supply and dispensed by only a few pharmacies, one of which happened to be in the man's town. The pharmacist, recognizing a chance to make tremendous profits, raised the price of the drug so high that the husband could not afford to buy it. The man wondered whether he should break into the store and steal the drug. Should he?

Here are five possible viewpoints.

   1. There is no need for deliberation. Stealing has been clearly prescribed for us as wrong.

2. It would be necessary to assign a numerical value to the husband's pleasure and the pharmacist's pain, and then the morality of the action could be decided.

3. The decision would be a painful one to make. The husband would recognize that he must obtain the drug. At the same time, he would know that breaking and entering are against the law and are punishable. If he did choose to steal, he would have to take the consequences.

4. The decision would a difficult one to make, for no doubt the pharmacist's profiteering could be considered as immoral as the theft itself.

5. Reason maintains that if stealing is wrong in one instance, it cannot be right in another.

In questions 27-31 below select the viewpoint with which each of the following would agree.

27. Bentham

28. devout Jew or Christian

29. situationalist

30. Socrates

31. existentialist

32. The term quixotic comes, as one might suppose, from the character Don Quixote, and serves to characterize someone who tends to be like Cervantes' great creation. If someone called you quixotic, they would probably mean that you were

   1. mathematically precise.
   2. an impractical idealist.
   3. filled with wit and good humor.
   4. a secular zealot.
   5. wrapped up in trivial details.

33. A problem moral philosophers have detected in existentialism is that

   1. it is not possible to have religious faith and still live an authentic life.
   2. if a person creates his own values, he will not perceive any action he has taken as morally wrong.
   3. the exercise of private conscience without reference to universal moral principles can lead to moral chaos.
   4. 1 and 2.
   5. 2 and 3.

34. Aristotle and the Utilitarians held in common the belief that

   1. the role of the state is to promote the happiness of the citizen.

92

2. the least government is the best for the happiness of the citizen.
3. happiness consists of satisfying every want.
4. any means employed to achieve a good end is morally permissible.
5. happiness is achieved by ridding oneself of greed for material possessions.

35. In both the Old and the New Testament the law is believed to be

   1. universally binding.
   2. a social contract subject to the will of the people.
   3. binding on the common people but not on rulers.
   4. imposed by a tyrannical deity.
   5. of societal origin.

36. One reason offered in the text for the apparent decline of moral values in the workplace is

   1. the breakdown of religion in modern times, resulting in a general climate of moral indifference.
   2. the separation of workers from the product of their work, as a result of mechanization.
   3. a resistance to secular zealotry on the part of most workers.
   4. the workers' recognition that industry exploits them.
   5. minorities' resentment of discrimination in the labor market.

MODULE VII

Philosophy: Eastern/Western Consciousness

OVERVIEW

Because the size of the globe is shrinking, the designations East and West no longer refer to geographical opposites so much as they do alternate belief patterns and ways of approaching life. Today many in the West look with great interest to the ancient philosophies of Hinduism and Buddhism, and many are finding there the basis for questioning, even altering value systems, particularly those rooted in traditional Western concepts: ego, individualism, fame and the importance of acquiring and owning. Though Hinduism and Buddhism have some profound differences-- particularly their divergent attitudes toward the existence of an absolute self--both schools of thought share the view that the purpose of life is not the attainment of worldly prestige and wealth by the individual. Rather, both see the pursuit of material gain as a vain quest of an illusion, and teach ways of becoming detached from the desires which this world continually seems to excite.

LEARNING OBJECTIVES

Having completed this module, you should be able to

1) present some broad differences other than geography which separate Eastern and Western approaches to life.

2) indicate some reasons for the present interest in Eastern thought and life-styles in Western society.

3) differentiate among Hinduism, mainstream Buddhism, Tibetan Buddhism, and Zen Buddhism.

4) discuss the emergence and characteristics of American Buddhism.

5) present some objections to Buddhist philosophies and life-styles advanced by Western critics.

6) determine what your own life-style might be if you were to introduce Buddhist elements into it.

95

Chapter 7: "Western Territory, Eastern Space"

1. What answers would be given to the following questions by a Hindu? By a Buddhist?
   a. What is the relationship between the human being and the natural world?
   b. What is the goal of human life?
   c. How may the goal be reached?

2. How does the Buddhist interpretation of nirvana differ from the Hindu?

3. How does the attitude toward karma differ in Hinduism and Buddhism?

4. Explain the Buddhist attitude toward ego-self. Why is the condition of ego-lessness essential to the attainment of enlightenment and the practice of ethical conduct?

5. How does the traditional Western definition of intelligence differ from the Buddhist use of the term?

6. Explain the importance of detachment and compassion in the Buddhist concept of self-worth and social concern.

7. Give evidence that Buddhist values are in conflict with other values in modern Japan.

8. What is meant by the "encounter with the Void" as a principle in Zen meditation? Why is this a difficult concept for the traditional Western approach to reality?

9. Account for the increase of American interest in Eastern values in the 60s.

10. What problems might typical Westerners encounter in attempting to incorporate Zen meditation into their lives?

11. Summarize the limitations of Western culture as seen from the viewpoint of Westerners who are choosing Eastern life styles.

12. Summarize some possible objections to Eastern practice that can be raised by the Western mind.

VIEWING

I. Territory and Space

   --The title of this program is symbolic, like its companion piece in this module. "Space" is a key word in Buddhism. Reality is vast, "spacious," without limits, beginnings, or ends. In contrast, "territory" is the goal of many people: a strong sense of self (or ego), the acquisition of material goods and properties, ownership of or power over other people, and so on.

--A major reason the young man is drawn to Buddhism is the value it places on non-aggressiveness. This is not to be understood as pacifism, but rather as the condition of total self-acceptance, which makes a person no longer defensive; defensiveness is in turn the source of agressive behavior, for many find that the only road to self-acceptance is to cause others to fail.

--In the opinion of some critics of Western values, the Western preoccupation with the purpose, function, and utility of natural things has given rise to the myth of human superiority to nature and has led to the present environmental and energy crises. By the same token, the romantic rapture over nature, characteristic of 19th century writings, may have inspired the assumption that somehow nature exists for humankind. In both the Buddhist and Taoist views, all being, whether human or natural, is one and the same. There is either being or not being. The variations in form, size, and complexity are of no greater importance than the difference in the size of individual leaves on a plant.

--Following the program titles, the narrator states that "Buddhists live in a world of circles." There is a double meaning here. First, there is much circular symbolism in Buddhism. There is, for example, the wheel of the Dharma mentioned by the narrator, a symbol of the perfect rightness of existence and of "the way" or "path," which becomes clear to those who devote themselves to meditation throughout their lives. But secondly, the phenomenon of living is itself circular in the sense that it never gets anywhere (quite the opposite of the Western emphasis on progress).

--The reference to the emptiness at the center of the circle is difficult for some Westerners to grasp. The Buddhist, through meditation, actually seeks emptiness, seeks to confront himself with the fundamental nothingness; for the belief is that, if you start with the premise of emptiness, you will not expect life to be anything in particular and thus you cannot be overwhelmed by suffering. Suffering comes from expecting life to have certain meanings and move in certain directions and from not being prepared to cope with whatever "moves" life may decide to make.

--The distinction is made between Buddhist meditation and Christian prayer. It is important to realize that meditation is not in any sense a form of prayer. While the various schools of Buddhism are sometimes termed religions, while they do have certain rituals which are important for group identification, the fundamental practice in Buddhism, meditation, contains no idea of a union between the meditator and any spiritual force or deity beyond him. The purpose of meditation is to learn how to exist in direct contact with immediate reality, whereas the purpose of prayer is to transcend one's surroundings and make contact with a higher reality.

--"The purpose of Buddhist meditation," says the narrator, "is to uncover the awakened state of mind, which is the expression of a centerless center." We have already established the fact that meditation brings the Buddhist to the "still and empty center." The question now is: "What do we mean by a center, and why is it centerless?" First, "center" means a point of conscious awareness. In the West we would call this the "self," but Buddhism objects to the word "self" because it suggests an entity that is complete and separate from all else. The Buddhist center is still in that it is free of passion; it is calm and detached. It is also centerless in that this point of conscious awareness is allowed to "float"--to be totally immersed in the reality of the

97

moment--as opposed to being aware of itself. Later in the program, Michael, the hero, experiences difficulty in being centerless. His mind insists on thinking its thoughts, so that Michael is not able simply to exist in a sitting position without entertaining himself through thought.

--The narrator, observing Michael's behavior and the reasons for his unhappiness, generalizes about certain forms of maladjustments which people in the West seem to exhibit. Her descriptions are presented visually and symbolically in a dance. According to her analysis, the main causes of suffering for the maladjusted Westerner are that they are pulled apart through over-involvement and they cannot exist discontinuously. They seek, she says, a "still center" (instead of the empty center of the program's title), meaning a coherence, an inner integration, which is for the Buddhist a mistaken, and impossible, goal.

--Michael leaves Colorado, because he cannot meditate "properly." He is still haunted by his family's (and society's) values. He believes there must be a proper, as opposed to improper, way of "doing Buddhism." He had hoped to be a success at that, without realizing that no such things as success and failure exist within the Buddhist outlook.

--But now, of course, his problem is that the job seems pointless to him. Why work so hard to distinguish oneself doing work that has no minute-by-minute satisfaction? Michael is "stuck" between East and West, one might say. He can exist partially in the moment, but then he keeps asking himself what he is doing there. He is still searching for some nameless goal.

--Michael's "enlightenment" takes place at his desk, and, in keeping with the theme of the centerless center, it is not very spectacular. One day all of the things that the narrator has been writing to him suddenly fall into place. He sits bolt upright, which is the meditation position, and looks calmly at every object on his desk, neither accepting nor rejecting, neither loving nor despising. He learns how simple it is to accept the moment in itself.

--In the next sequence we find Michael absorbed in the details of his job, with a smile on his face. What do you think has happened to him? Is he "resigned" to his lot? Is he now inspired by his job? What is the secret...which is really not a secret at all?"

SELF-TEST

T 1.   Buddhists differ from   the enlightened one   _____
        Christians and Moslems...
                                       beginnings of sitting meditation   _____
T 2.   Buddhism grew out of
                                       egolessness   _____
VT 3.   success and failure
                                       Eightfold Path   _____
T 4.   Bodhi tree
                                       desperate search for personal goal   _____
T 5.   true condition of human
        life, according to Buddhism   humanity is superior to the   _____
                                       rest of the natural world
T 6.   right view, right
        intentions, etc.   to a Buddhist, only feelings   _____
                                       about oneself
V 7.   Michael's problem
                                       Hindu traditions and religion   _____
V 8.   Michael's enlightenment
                                       no belief in godhead   _____
VT 9.   territory, as opposed to
        space   the need to possess   _____

T 10.   Bodhisattva   preparation for Buddhahood   _____

T 11.   Siddhartha Guatama   clearsigned acceptance   _____
                                       of all things
V 12   a Western assumption

99

CHECK LIST OF MAIN IDEAS

1. Eastern beliefs differ appreciably from those of the West and offer to many Westerners a viable alternative life style, one in which there is far less stress on the importance of individual achievement and material gains.

2. In this module, two important Eastern religions are discussed. Hinduism: based on the premise that one must live through many cycles of birth and rebirth before one achieves a purity of soul allowing one to enter nirvana, a state in which life's suffering is eliminated. One's position in life directly reflects virtues or vices exhibited in one's previous existence. Buddhism: founded on the teachings of Siddhartha Guatama who discovered that nirvana was neither a heavenly abode nor death, but a totally awakened state in which one views life with compassionate detachment.

3. Zen Buddhism is a Japanese practice which aims at enlightenment through intensive meditation, even to a monastic withdrawal from the affairs of daily life.

4. Tibetan Buddhism, the most popular strain in the United States today, believes less in the uniqueness of the Buddha than in buddha-nature or buddha-mind, which is universal and exists potentially in everyone.

CURRENTS FROM EASTERN WATERS

by

Joan Cronin

CONTRASTS IN CONSCIOUSNESS

The culture traditionally considered Western inherits--from classical Greece and the Old Testament--an underlying concept of duality in all existence. God and man are separate realities, as are man and nature, body and mind. In like fashion our individual egos separate us from other people and give each of us a sense of uniqueness. We take pride in the progress made possible by our rational intelligence: the conquest of disease, the harnessing of natural power, the steadily expanding system of information about the universe. And we write books and erect monuments to live after us in defeat of death and oblivion.

Buddhism sees life and death as part of the continuous flow of existence. It denies that there is any duality. There is only existence, and it is totally present in every manifestation of being, whether it is a man or a bird or a pebble in the stream. Buddhism offers a unifying vision, reached by quieting the busy ego-mind and attaining intuitive sources of wisdom. What is important is not to seek success but to live in the present moment with total awareness, to accept with quiet mind whatever is.

This apparent emphasis on passivity and this refusal to deify the rational mind or to engage in competitive striving seems uncomfortable to many energetic Westerners; yet many others claim to have found in the Buddhist approach a source of tranquility, self-acceptance, and enhanced awareness even as they continue to lead busy, active lives. They believe it is possible to effect a synthesis of both Buddhist and Western orientations to life.

THE TAO

Another unifying concept central to much Eastern culture is contained in Taoism, a philosophy that originated in China in the 6th centurty before Christ and has influenced the thinking of a number of American writers and artists.

Tao is almost impossible to translate in words. It means something like the Way, a formless, eternal principle that flows through all existence and in which all things participate. The Tao is not a thing, but it is not nothingness either.

101

The joyous life is one lived in harmony with the Tao. This quality of existence is achieved by the practice of wu wei, that is a state of quietude that is not really inactive but a source of creative energy. The Chinese philosopher Lao-Tzu (who is credited with founding Taoism and writing the Tao Te Ching, sometimes translated as The Way of Power), made an analogy between this state of wu wei and the qualities we are all familiar with in water. Water effortlessly bears things up and carries them along. One who understands the Tao knows that it, like water, will sustain him if he does not flail about and rebel against the fundamental order of things. Like the Tao, the gentle power of water can smooth rocks into pebbles and melt away mountains. In the social order, leaders who have mastered this gentle power can rule without force or strident argument. Finally, water attains clarity by standing still, permitting the debris to settle. Thus one does well to wait in quiet for mental distractions to dissipate if one would finally attain clear consciousness.

To the Taoist, assertiveness and competition go counter to the Way. We would not be agressive toward other people, or toward the natural world, if we followed the Tao in which all participate. This feeling for the totality of existence had a strong influence on the landscape painters of the Sung period in medieval China, and its influence continues among many modern artists. In such paintings the human figures blend quietly with the natural background and are very small in the overall perspective. A general mistiness often obliterates the distinctions between forms, and everything flows together with the utmost harmony.

HINDUISM: OLD AND NEW

The concept of Tao is expressed as Dharma in both Hinduism and Buddhism. Here too it signifies a universal order. But for the Hindu this order was not always a source of joy and well-being as it was for the Taoist. In the earlier history of India, the idea of Dharma operating in the social order permitted the development of a rigid caste system. The highest castes kept as their privileged possession the sacred writings that taught the Way of justice and virtue. Thus the lower castes could not know what they needed to, in order to avoid wrongdoing. To work off the consequences of their inevitable errors, they saw themselves doomed to an endless series of reincarnations, in each lifetime suffering the consequences of the previous one and accumulating more Karma (the inescapable effects of deeds). They longed to be released from the painful round of life, death, and rebirth; to be absorbed in nirvana, into Brahman, the eternel World Soul. But there was an element of near hopelessness in early Hinduism, for such release could be attained only by the elite castes, and it might take an ordinary person eons of time to work his way up from one lifetime to another.

However, important changes took place in Hinduism in more recent times. During the 19th century, a reform movement known as Ramakrishna began in India. It combined a mystical faith with active concern for human needs. The Ramakrishna group has been responsible for the building of orphanages, hospitals, schools, and universities; it now has work centers all over India and in many of the world's great cities. Mahatma Gandhi, the chief figure of modern Hinduism, exemplifies in his life the doctrine of non-violence and the social concern implicit in the Ramakrishna movement.

The Hindu belief that desire, the cause of suffering, is the fruit of ignorance was absorbed into Buddhism, which was founded by Siddhartha Gautama in the 6th century before Christ. But Gautama's experience of enlightenment brought to Buddhism a far more optimistic possibility: nirvana is attainable, at least theoretically, for everyone, for the knowledge of the Dharma is revealed not in sacred writings but in

102

meditation on the Four Noble Truths and Holy Eightfold Path, which is really a practical course in systematic habit formation. It has been called the path of common sense, in which one avoids suffering by choosing the middle-way between the extremes, for instance, of self-indulgence and self-denial. Through meditation and following the way of the Buddha Dharma, even the simplest person could hope to achieve enlightenment, that is, nirvana.

BUDDHISM: HINAYANA AND MAHAYANA

However, in practice it was not always so. The earliest form of Buddhism, called the Hinayana, or Narrow Path, taught that nirvana could be attained only if one became a monk, for it was thought impossible to meditate and follow the Path while living an active life in the world, which was full of distractions and temptations. Thus again nirvana was possible only for a limited number, and for them nirvana meant personal salvation with no active concern for the welfare of others.

The Mahayana, or Broad Path, a later form of Buddhism still practiced in both East and West, asserts that salvation (enlightenment) is universally attainable. One who seeks Buddha-mind need not be a monk, but can hope to attain enlightenment while living the everyday life of the world. At one stage a Bodhisattva (of future Buddha) becomes a "great cosmic helper," dedicated to helping mankind to find release. In this way Mahayana Buddhism contains a more humane ethic than Hinayana, and at the heart of that ethic is the quality of compassionate detachment. A Buddhist's conduct--toward himself or his environment or the people he lives and works among--is measured by this quality, for without it, it is impossible to follow the Eightfold Path to enlightenment.

ZEN

Zen is a form of Buddhism that places very strong emphasis on intensive, long periods of meditation as the gateway to the harmony of the Way. By learning through discipline to free the mind of ego-distraction and drawing upon the intuitive wisdom everyone is born with, one can learn to live, attentive to what is going on in the reality of the moment. Some schools of Zen insist upon an almost monastic withdrawal for meditation, but throughout the West there has been a growth of Zen centers, where people live and meditate together, even while holding a variety of jobs outside.

THE JAPANESE SENSE OF THE BEAUTIFUL

The meditative approach to life that attracts so many people in the West has also produced a uniquely Japanese sense of the beautiful that is evident in many

---

Tea and Tantra

Tea Ceremony is a journey into ourselves - in and out again. We travel alone with others also alone. We bow, we bend. Bowing "In Tea" is not just a matter of politeness. It is a way of yielding to the mystery of being human.

--Milly Johnstone

103

aspects of life. The tea ceremony (known as Cha No Ya or The Way of Tea) is both a meditative and an esthetic experience. It was designed some five hundred years ago by Rikuyo as a way of harmonizing his practical business mind with the awareness he achieved in sitting meditation. The tea ceremony remains much the same today as Rikuyo created it.

When a guest enters the tea hut, he finds tranquil refreshment for each of his senses. He is greated by a subtle aroma of incense, a sound of water boiling, a beautiful vase or a simple flower arrangement in a corner. Host and guest bow respectfully. The host prepares the tea, and they sip it, savoring its delicacy. Like all Japanese meals, tea is taken slowly and quietly, and flavors are subtle, even bland. It is not at all like an American meal, where, ideally, brilliant table talk and well-defined flavors create a bright, exciting atmosphere. The host and guest may remain silent throughout the Japanese tea ceremony, or they may converse quietly, admiring some beautiful object in the room like the bowl in which the tea is served. The beauty of the object may not be immediately apparent; the tea bowl may be a plain old one, cracked and mended with gold. What makes it precious is the quality of sabi, a preference for what is simple--even poor--over the pretentious and luxurious. Sabi involves too, an awareness
ness of the perishableness of all things
The old tea bowl is beautiful because it
speaks of our mortality, and does so
with concrete immediacy.

> If man were never to fade away like the dews of Adahino, never to vanish like the smoke over Torobeyana, but linger on forever in the world, how things would lose their power to move us! The most precious thing in life is its uncertainty.
>
> --Kendo

Japanese art forms, like the Haiku (a short verse form) and the traditional brush painting, also illustrate the tranquil, meidative approach to life. The haiku poet is confined to exactly seventeen syllables; he writes of a fragmentary, fleeting moment and relies on a minute concrete detail to communicate somehow the totality of the experience. To appreciate such stark simplicity requires a willingness in the reader to admit that more exists than can ever be put into words. The poet Basho write of his desire to make the deepest possible contact with the very center of life. To do this he felt, one must observe minute aspects of things in nature, the seen and the heard, as if there were no separation between them and himself.

> Winter desolation;
> In a world of one
> color.
> The sound of the
> wind.
> --Basho

Japanese brush painting has many of the qualities of the haiku. In a few swift strokes the artist may depict a bird or a snowladen branch. That is all of the picture. The viewer is invited to participate with his imagination, to create with the artist. The effect in both these art forms is one of spontaneity and spaciousness, of essential truth caught with the greatest simplicity and directness.

> The Way of Haiku arises from concentration and lack of distraction. Look well within yourself.
>
> --Basho

The visitor to a Japanese garden finds a similar experience. A mood of meditative quiet is achieved by the apparently artless arrangement of a single tree, a rock, a slow drip of water from a bamboo pipe. The imagination is given infinite space to create the whole forest, the mountain, the waterfall. No brilliant flower beds distract the eye or the mind. Simplicity, naturalness, a sense of space and tranquillity achieved with apparently effortless ease are all qualities that contrast sharply with the ideal of beauty one would find in the formal gardens of Europe, where the visitor's eye is regaled with avenues of statues, polite flower beds, and sculptured shrubbery. At Versailles, for instance, one feels that beauty is achieved by the construction of sharply defined areas, not by the experience of space.

Generally speaking, then, the Japanese attitude toward beauty shares with the meditative approach to life a feeling for quiet harmony with the natural world, for the reality contained in each brief moment and for the mystery underlying existence that cannot be rationally apprehended.

RECOMMENDED READING

The Bhagavad Gita. An epic poen containing the dialogs of a warrior and his charioteer Krishna, an incarnation of the Hindu god Vishnu.

Edward Conze. Buddhist Scriptures (Baltimore: Penguin Books, 1959). An accurate, poetic, and highly readable translation of major Buddhist sacred writings containing a picturesque account of the Buddha's enlightenment.

Hermann Hesse. Siddhartha tr. Hilda Rusner (New York: New Directions, 1951). A story not of the historic Buddha but of a wealthy young Brahmin who seeks spiritual fulfillment, meets the Buddha, only to be disillusioned by him, and eventually to become aware that the Buddha nature can only be found in oneself.

Lao-Tzu. The Way of Life (Appears in various translations and editions). A series of exquisite poems each of which succinctly conveys a simple yet complex insight into some aspect of living (e.g., the way of life is soft, the way of death is hard).

D. T. Suzuki. Essays in Zen Buddhism (New York: Grove Press, 1961). Highly readable essays on various aspects of the philosophy and practice of Zen directed at Western consciousness. Of particular interest is the description of the relationship between Zen master and student.

Chögyum Trongpa. The Myth of Freedom (Berkeley: Shambhala, 1976). A compilation of Buddhist teachings addressed to American sensibilities by a foremost Tibetan guru.

Alan Watts. Nature, Man, and Woman (New York: Pantheon, 1958). The foremost Western spokesman for Zen Buddhism contrasts Eastern and Western beliefs and values in the matter of sexual identity and relationships.

MODULE VIII

Critical Thinking

(NOTE: This module relates to Chapters 8 and 9 of the text. The two films: The
Wonder of Form and Phoenix and Finnegan relate to both chapters.)

OVERVIEW

The critical habit of mind is a uniquely human trait, one that can and ought to
be developed by anyone who hopes to make the most of living. Critical thinkers can
usually be distinguished from noncritical people by their willingness to concentrate
on the issues at hand, to weigh the facts and see them in context, to judge fairly
and dispassionately. They are able to see past particulars to broad patterns and
principles. Since they often perceive matters in a figurative light, they are able
to bring humor and imagination to the solving of both personal and community
problems.

The skills involved in analytical thought are accessible to all kinds of people.
One way to master this valuable process is to practice the techniques of professional
critics of the arts. By learning from them to distinguish such things as historical
contexts, artistic genres, and assumptions about esthetic principles, we can all
develop confidence in our own judgment and heighten our power to see and hear the
world.

LEARNING OBJECTIVES

Having completed this module, you should be able to

1) enumerate elements in the art of critical thinking.

2) explain some advantages of being a critical thinker.

3) give some examples of critical thinkers at work.

4) differentiate between literalists and figuratists.

5) explain what is meant by critical perspective and discuss the means by
    which it can be attained.

6) identify and evaluate the various theories about the function of art
    advanced by Plato, Congreve, Swift, Tolstoy, and Orwell.

7) state the tenets of the "art for art's sake" school of criticism.

8) argue for or against the theory that moral censorship ought to be applied
    to works of art.

107

9) explain in your own words what a critic might mean by pointing out that a
    given work is lacking in "form."

10) illustrate a relationship that a critic might make between the life and the
    art of James Joyce.

AS YOU READ

Chapter 8: "On Being a Critical Thinker"

1. The chapter makes a basic distinction between critical and noncritical people.
    It points out that the latter tend to be so thoroughly absorbed in their own
    world that they fail to observe the shape of experience. We may also conclude
    that the humanities help us to develop that observation.

2. Summarize Carl Sagan's "three-brain" theory. Presumably all three operate
    within us. Give additional examples of the older brains at work.

3. Some people believe that an emotional approach to solving their problems shows
    more "humanness" than does an analytical approach. Discuss the weakness in this
    theory.

4. What are some major roadblocks to critical thinking?

5. The chapter indicates that each of us is capable of operating on three different
    levels of consciousness. What are they? Does it matter if we fail to strike a
    balance among them?

6. Be able to sum up effective steps to take in problem solving.

7. How may it be an advantage to be a critical thinker? Are there any occupations
    in which critical thinking would not be important?

8. The critical thinker is someone who goes beyond the specific instance to a
    general principle. What does this mean, and why is the ability a crucial one?

9. Contrast literalists and figuratists. Does the literalist labor under any
    significant disadvantages in life?

10. What is personalizing? How does personalizing affect conversation? An adequate
    review of an art exhibit, concert or dramatic work?

11. What do you suppose Paul Goodman meant when he said that most of us grow up
    "absurd"?

12. Identify elements of the professional critic's art that the general public can
    use to extend their understanding and enjoyment of the arts.

Chapter 9: "Critical Thinking and the Arts"

1. Explain what is meant by the statement that Robert Brustein is a philosophical critic. In what ideas does he resemble Aristotle?

2. How can you tell which reviewers not to trust?

3. A responsible and competent reviewer judges by a variety of criteria which differ from one art form to another. What elements would you expect to see evaluated, for instance, in a classical tragedy? or a new Broadway play? or a Hitchcock movie thriller?

4. What steps can one take to develop a critical perspective in the arts? How does "genre awareness" assist in this process?

5. Can a case be made for morality-based censorship of the arts? Be prepared to discuss the pros and cons of the question.

6. What criteria does Tolstoy insist upon in judging a work to be great art?

The two films which accompany this module do not at first appear to have much in common. The Wonder of Form examines various meanings of the word "form" as it relates to the humanities, from Plato's celebrated theory of Form to specific kinds of forms we can observe in the arts of differing periods. The film ultimately focuses on the major differences between classical and modern forms and why they occurred.

It can be explicated in and for itself as a guide to the understanding of the ancient and the modern worlds. But the intention behind the film was also to have the student viewers experience form in the making by becoming aware of the circular structure. The program begins and ends with the sea, but by the ending the viewer is expected to have attained an insight into why we humans are so fascinated with the sea. That is, in the alternation between the rising and falling of the tides, we find an analogy to alternating aspects of our own selves--to the classical in us, which seeks permanence, a haven from the restless sea, and to the modern in us, which dislikes permanence and is always looking to new adventures. Coming to see the form in the film itself, finally, illustrates how the critical thinker should respond to this program.

Phoenix and Finnegan, in contrast, concentrates on the life and art of a great twentieth-century writer, James Joyce--in particular, how he took the subject matter of a rowdy barroom ballad and turned it into one of the cornerstone achievements in modern literature: Finnegans Wake. In this film we have an illustration of how the truly perceptive critical mind seeks to understand a given work by finding out as much as possible about how it came to be written. Not all works lend themselves to so-called "biographical criticism," but Finnegans Wake assuredly does. In addition, the film illustrates the effort of the critic to humanize the artist and place his work squarely in the day-to-day real experiences of real people.

The Wonder of Form

--"To discover the ultimate order behind all things has long been a human dream." We credit Plato with being the first to theorize in a rational way about the ultimate order behind creation. Plato postulates a realm of ideas, eternal and changeless, behind the multitudinous and continually changing forms of the actual world. For example, the ideal of "treeness," he says, exists behind all the forms of tree and gives to them their generic character. It is so with everything in the universe. It is as if the Divine Mind contained a blueprint of which the material world is an imperfect set of variations.

--Plato's theory will strike some as a fanciful, even an absurd explanation of the world. Yet some contemporary psychologists tend to substantiate Plato when they assert that models or archetypes (the name archetype means first model) of forms, life situations, states of mind, and so forth, are inherent in the mind and do shape our perceptions of the world. For example, when people in different parts of the world and in different cultures are asked to draw their idea of "bird," the results are virtually the same--something that has "birdness" and that everyone can recognize. We have seen how Paleolithic man painted bison, mammoths, and deer that in form, movement, and vitality have never been excelled. We know how important it was for the hunter-artist to make his animals real. But what happened when he drew men? He made them as

110

matchstick figures--for all the world as a three-year old would. Why? Did his
talents falter when it came to the human figure? Not likely. Or did he simply
not concern himself with "reality" in this instance, but only with the abstract
idea of "humanness?" One can't dispute that the quality of "humanness" is
there; even a child couldn't miss it.

--"The principle of harmony found in many of the world's great works of art is
sometimes called the classical principle." It is the formal, harmonious,
balanced interrelationship among lines, colors, textures, and parts of a work.
"The classical statue suggests the fixed and eternal," as if it manifested
universal law. Classicism's effect is one of serenity, of purity, and elevation
of spirit. How is it then that other works, of equal greatness, reject the
classical principle and seek to affect us in a different way: to arouse us, to
initiate inner movement, to intensify our physical perceptions--of eye, or ear,
or touch? The terms classical and modern are more than historical labels,
representing opposite sides of our nature--compensatory sides, if you will--both
necessary for an esthetic perception of the world.

--"The artist is the person who seeks to bring the ideal down into this world. . .
to freeze a moment of eternity." Artists often have the conviction that they
are engaged in discovering what already exists. . . in nature; perhaps, in the
mind of God. The Greeks liked to speak of the artist's enthusiasm--a word
composed of en, meaning "in", and theos, meaning "god." Michelangelo held the
belief that his sculptured forms were imprisoned inside the marble as ideas
waiting to be released. It was his tragic fate never to feel that he had
realized the Divine Idea implicit there. . . only an imperfect representation.

Phoenix and Finnegan

--This presentation constitutes a departure in both concept and style from the
rest of the programs in this series. In the first place, it is concerned
entirely with the life and work of a single literary figure: the Irish writer
James Joyce. In this respect it is the one pointedly "literary" unit in the
series. Its focus, however, lies elsewhere. The subject of the program is not
Joyce's characteristics as a literary genius, but rather Joyce as a symbol of
the human capacity to transcend despair and nihilism. Out of the ashes of
profound cynicism Joyce created a 20th century mythology that exalts the human
spirit. If much modern literature speaks of death, Joyce's major work shouts
resurrection.

--Two major symbols are employed in this program to structure and focus the
content: the legend of the Phoenix, and the mock-heroic legend of Tim Finnegan's
rise, fall, death, and resurrection. By and large, these symbols are dealt with
not directly, but by narrative indirection.

--The Phoenix, a mythical bird, was supposed in ancient times to live in some
remote part of the world--some said Arabia, others said Egypt or India. It was
the only bird of its kind, and it lived an incredible number of years. When its
time came to die, it returned to the place of its birth, consumed itself in
flames, then rose again from its own ashes, renewed and splendid.

--The Phoenix idea has long served as a metaphor or model for all forms of self-
renewal. In its most epic form, it symbolizes the cyclic processes of human
life--the long, slow swell of history with its recurrent patterns, the rhythmic

111

rise and fall of generations, the power of the human spirit to revitalize itself again and again.

--Although the figure of the Phoenix is not explicitly featured in this program, its presence is to be understood and felt--in the underlying ideas drawn from James Joyce's two masterworks: Ulysses and Finnegans Wake

--Ulysses or Odysseus was the man who left his remote island kingdom of Ithaca, fought at Troy, roamed the known world, endured uncounted hardships and the enmity of gods, and then at last found his way back home, to his own hearthfire, his faithful wife, his friends, fields and vineyards--everything that was waiting there to be renewed, to called back to life. In Joyce's version of the myth, the Ulysses figure, Leopold Bloom, a Dublin Jew, shares with his Greek predecessor the quality of being a displaced person; for like Homer's hero, who was always a stranger in the lands he visited, Bloom does not fit into the Irish mainstreams. Yet survive he does.

--The bartender/narrator notes that with Ulysses, Joyce began to dissect the English language in earnest, and to put it back together again in a form which baffled many readers (a bewilderment which was to be eclipsed by the stupor with which these same readers greeted Finnegans Wake a decade later). We have not the space for a full discussion of Joycean linguistics, but the student should be aware that in his need to explore the mysterious country of the unconscious mind and to transfer its complexities to paper, Joyce could not use conventional words or grammatical structure. Relative to the theme of this module, which covers both death attitudes and life-affirming strategies, we can regard Joyce's creation of a new language and a new grammar as another type of resurrection--the liberation of artistic imagination from the shackles of traditional communication.

--The structure of Finnegans Wake is that of a dream--the actual dream of Humphrey Chimpden Earwicker asleep above his Dublin pub, and the symbolic dream of mankind's history--archetypal, freighted with all the mythic meaning it has gathered along the way. The nucleus of the dream is the popular ballad "Finnegan's Wake," the story of Tim Finnegan, who after dying from a fall was given a splendid wake by his cronies--in the proper Irish spirit, of course, with plenty of food, plenty of drink, and plenty of fighting. In the melee someone spills whiskey on the corpse, and Tim rises from his bier, even as the Phoenix bird had risen from its own ashes through thousands of mythological years.

--Under Joyce's hands, the ballad of "Finnegan's Wake" is transformed, in widening circles, into a universal resurrection myth, and Tim Finnegan emerges as a fabulous prehistoric hero. Later, after a thunderous fall and death, he is resurrected as H. C. Earwicker the pub-keep, whose night-long dream, constituting the novel, traverses the whole of man's mythic world. In the cyclic pattern, Earwicker also suffers a fall--in of all places, Phoenix Park, Dublin--and we are back again with our first symbol.

SELF-TEST A

Match each item in the first column with an item in the second. Use no item more than once.

T 1.   reptilian brain   literalists   _____

V 2.   modernism   analysis leading to evaluation   _____

T 3.   Immanuel Kant   moral principles are universally   _____
                                      binding
T 4.   tend to be figurative
                                      beauty is a Form   _____
V 5.   Plato
                                      developed survival techniques   _____
T 6.   <u>Brave New World</u>
                                      critical thinkers   _____
T 7.   respond to parts rather
       than whole patterns   welcomes experiment and change   _____

V 8.   the classical principle   society governed by programmed   _____
                                      thinkers

T 9.   analogy   an unsafe basis for moral judgment   _____

T 10. criticism   order and permanence   _____

SELF-TEST B

T 1.   The Godfather

V 2.   James Joyce

V 3.   Robert Brustein

T 4.   Aristotle

T 5.   George Orwell

T 6.   Jonathan Swift

T 7.   Leo Tolstoy

V 8.   Ulysses

T 9.   William Congreve

V 10.   Finnegan

denounced as pornographic ravings of a madman   _____

function of art is to give sweetness and light   _____

denounced by some critics as morally dangerous   _____

the function of art is the betterment of life   _____

called the world's first critic   _____

said the playwright should mirror his time   _____

found inspiration in people once considered sinful and fallen subject of drinking song and myth   _____

rejected "artsakist" criticism   _____

described as philosopher/critic   _____

CHECK LIST OF MAIN IDEAS

1. Professional critics generally agree that there is a universal standard of excellence in the arts, even though some people will claim that it's a matter of personal taste.

2. Professional critics are necessary to society as guides to good taste.

3. We can all develop critical perspective by making a habit of reading responsible critical reviews, understanding the qualities of particular genres, and using the techniques of critical thinking discussed in Chapter 8.

4. Professional critics have at times assumed the role of guardian of public morality. The question is raised of whether the critic ought to have the power to censor the content of a work of art. The "art for art's sake" critic argues that the content of a work of art has no significance in itself. Others however, believe that antisocial subject matter can affect public morality and should be critically discouraged.

5. Critical thinking in the context of the humanities does not imply a negative attitude but rather an informed analysis that takes place before one makes a judgment. Critical thinking is a process that is possible for anyone to learn.

6. There is a widespread conviction that people who are guided by their feelings in making important decisions are somehow better human beings than those who rely on deliberate, rational thought processes; however, it is evident that the real problems we face every day are not resolved by emotional impulses.

7. By developing some of the skills of the professional critics, we can all enhance our experience of the arts.

8. Critical thinkers are more likely to be figuratists than literalists.

9. The critical thinker is objective, analytical, empathetic, often playful, not self-centered, and likely to exhibit a high talent for language.

RECOMMENDED READING

Robert Brustein. <u>Seasons of Discontent</u> (New York: Simon and Schuster, 1965). A
   classic statement from a major twentieth century critic, defending critical
   elitism and reaffirming the classical view of the critic as the guardian of
   public taste.

Aaron Copland. <u>What to Listen for in Music</u> (New York: McGraw-Hill, 1957). One of
   the greatest of American composers helps us, through a series of extremely lucid
   essays, to hear better what instruments, melodic lines, and harmonic patterns
   are saying to us.

Alexandra Danilova. <u>Choura, the Memoirs of Alexandra Danilova</u> (New York: Knopf,
   1986). A highly entertaining autobiography of one of the great dancers of our
   time. This should be read by anyone who would like to develop a more critical
   appreciation of ballet and modern dance.

Richard Friedenthal, ed. <u>Letters of the Great Artists</u> (New York: Random House, 1963)
   2 vols. This superb collection offers tremendous insights into the intentions
   of great visual artists. Recommended to those who want to become intelligent
   critical viewers.

Plato. <u>The Republic</u> (See Recommended Reading, Module VI). Part VII, containing the
   "Allegory of the Cave," is of most particular interest because it offers Plato's
   most famous presentation of his theory of the Forms.

Kathleen Tynan. <u>The Life of Kenneth Tynan</u> (New York: William Morrow, 1987). A
   biography of the famous British drama critic written by his wife, revealing an
   interesting contrast between the sometimes controversial life of the man and the
   absolute integrity of his critical standards.

Survey 4

1. Which of the following options represents the <u>best</u> explanation for the current
   interest in Buddhism in Western society?

   1. the teachings of the Dalai Lama recently translated
   2. the communist purge of Buddhists in China and Tibet
   3. a questioning of the success/failure orientation
   4. the growing fear that there is not enough time left to enjoy the pleasure
      of the senses
   5. a dissatisfaction with standardized living and a need for an escape from
      everyday, humdrum reality

2. Buddhism broke away from Hinduism because of a profound difference over one
   major issue. Which of the following represents the Buddhist view of the matter?

   1. Enlightenment is attainable in the course of a single lifetime.
   2. Enlightenment is allowed to one individual in each eon of time, and he is
      called "Buddha."
   3. One must reach the Brahmin class through the cycles of birth and rebirth
      before one is eligible for enlightenment.
   4. The meditation process must be carried out through the chanting of once
      unspoken mantras.
   5. The holy teacher is no longer important; each person interprets scripture
      for himself.

3. In the TV program <u>Territory and Space</u> which of the following contrasts was <u>not</u>
   made?

   1. the territorial imperative and egolessness
   2. competitiveness and nonaggression
   3. Christ and Buddha
   4. Buddha, before and after enlightenment
   5. manipulation of the environment and living on nature's terms

4. At the conclusion of <u>The Still and Empty Center</u> Michael has apparently found a
   way to synthesize Eastern and Western elements into his way of life. Which of
   the following statements best characterizes Michael's life at this point?

   1. He will continue to work in his father's business but will be contemptuous
      of it.

117

2. He has recognized that the need to get ahead is too basic to his nature to struggle against it.
3. He will leave the business and enter a zendo.
4. He has discovered that the wakeful state can be achieved anywhere.
5. He is willing to sacrifice his Buddhist ambitions for his parents' sake.

5. In the Hindu religion, deities are actually personifications of natural forces. Brahma is a personification of

   1. war.
   2. knowledge.
   3. the ego.
   4. creativity.
   5. death.

6. Tibetan Buddhism departs from mainstream Buddhism in that it doesn't include

   1. perpetual homage to the one true Buddha.
   2. emphasis on the potential Buddha-nature of all people.
   3. the belief that more than one Buddha is possible in any given age.
   4. the practice of sitting meditation.
   5. egolessness.

7. A man asked of the wise one: "What is the truth?" The wise one promptly answered: "Then you will never understand." Which of the following approaches to living would be most likely to teach its principles through such anecdotes?

   1. Zen Buddhism
   2. Tibetan Buddhism
   3. Hinduism
   4. Dharmadhatu
   5. Vajradhatu

8. Buddhist meditation is a technique for

   1. overcoming pain by practicing mind-over-matter.
   2. denying one's sensations, emotions, and thoughts.
   3. tuning in to the subtle sensations of the flesh.
   4. transcending the wakeful state through a mystic union.
   5. achieving the wakeful state.

9. Unlike Buddhists, Hindus believe that the universe is an expression of

   1. an absolute self.
   2. futility.
   3. desire.
   4. nirvana.
   5. detachment.

10. The following statements all express well-known moral attitudes. One is most congenial to the Buddhist philosophy. Which is it?

    1. You do your thing, I'll do mine.

2. Do your thing as long as you don't hurt anyone.
3. No man is an island.
4. Different strokes for different folks.
5. Do unto others as you would have them do unto you.

11. Critics of the spread of Buddhism in the West are likely to cite which of the following arguments as a means of discrediting those who dedicate themselves to Buddhist practice?

   1. Buddhism actually makes one more competitive and aggressive.
   2. Buddhism is a conspiracy for world domination.
   3. Buddhism is really based on self-interest, even though it purports to deemphasize the self.
   4. Buddhism works best in countries where the individual counts for little.
   5. Both 1 and 3 are correct.

12. One of the following Buddhist elements you might be able to introduce into your present way of life; which one would probably cause the least interruption of a typically Western existence?

   1. the overcoming of a need for money and status
   2. an intensive dedication to Zen practice
   3. achieving enlightenment in the manner of Gautama
   4. setting aside a certain length of time each day for sitting practice
   5. following the example of Bodhidharma

13. To Buddhists, when one frees oneself from the illusion of ego, which of the following disappears?

   1. mind-chatter
   2. the Void
   3. nirvana
   4. tranquility
   5. detachment

14. Americans, we are told by Michael's dance teacher, seek a still, unchanging center. Presumably this ideal center is not an empty one. What is she saying that Americans seek?

   1. an integrated, tranquil life
   2. egolessness
   3. philosophical alternatives to certainty
   4. rebellion against traditionalism
   5. perpetual youth

15. The Still and Empty Center shows a young man's search for a satisfying way of life. His initial efforts to master the Buddhist way are not very successful, because

   1. he discovers that he lacks a spiritual dedication.
   2. the Buddhist teachers refuse to grant enlightenment to an American.
   3. he lacks a background in Hindu scriptures and prophecies.
   4. he brings with him Western standards of accomplishment.

5. since he has been a teacher himself, he will not open himself to learn from others.

16. Which of the following is not a suggested step in applying critical thinking to problem solution?

    1. Find out if there is a problem.
    2. Find out whether there are any choices.
    3. Determine whose problem it is.
    4. Examine assumptions.
    5. Get in touch with your gut feelings.

17. One of the major obstacles to critical thinking is the tendency to

    1. abstract.
    2. personalize.
    3. make comparisons.
    4. find paradoxes.
    5. question assumptions.

18. The point is made that when nonprofessionals apply critical analysis to an art work,

    1. they discourage the artist because they think that criticism is a negative statement.
    2. the criticism is probably bad since the general public can't know what criteria to apply.
    3. they can intensify their esthetic pleasure in the art work.
    4. they usually reject universal standards of taste in favor of personalized, relative criteria.
    5. they are not really thinking critically because they are judging by the commercial success of the work.

19. The most successful way for students to take an essay exam would be to

    1. get lots of sleep first.
    2. rely on the promptings of the right hemisphere of the brain.
    3. analyze what the question is asking them to do.
    4. tell all they know about the subject; something relevant is bound to emerge.
    5. substitute what they do know for what is asked; anything is better than a blank space.

20. "Outstanding athletes should be judged by different standards from other people." This statement is offered as an example of

    1. a common sense solution to a moral problem.
    2. a moral dilemma.
    3. the superiority of moral judgment made from compassion over one made from rigid principle.
    4. an argument from false analogy.
    5. a failure to match a concrete example to a universal principle.

21. Which of the following statements is not usually true of literalists?

1. They concentrate on concrete details rather than on general principles.
2. They are concerned with themselves rather than with the subject at hand.
3. They perceive fragments rather than whole patterns.
4. Their language is often colorful and imaginative.
5. They tend to digress from the subject.

22. Buddhists would agree with behavioral psychologists that the desire to accumulate territory is

   1. a basic instinct in all animals.
   2. a universal source of unhappiness.
   3. an attitude acquired from one's culture.
   4. necessary for survival in a capitalist society.
   5. all of the above.

23. In Buddhism the Dharma is

   1. the cycle of rebirth.
   2. the emancipation from the cycle of birth, death, and rebirth.
   3. the futility of a life lived to satisfy temporal desires.
   4. the burden of accumulated guilt acquired in a lifetime.
   5. the moral structure underlying all existence.

24. All but one are characteristics of critical thinking. Which one is not?

   1. a figurative habit of mind
   2. a willingness to admit error
   3. disinterested evaluation
   4. the tendency to reach immediate conclusions
   5. the perception of whole patterns

25. The "middle" or mammalian brain probably originated in

   1. need for locomotive control.
   2. respect for the chain of command.
   3. family instinct.
   4. the need for critical analysis.
   5. the need for symbolic activity.

26. The chapter on critical thinking makes the point that

   1. we are all born with an instinct for critical thinking; all we need in order to exercise it is self-confidence.
   2. people who rely on their feelings in difficult situations are more trustworthy than those who operate analytically.
   3. critical thinking is not a skill all normal people can develop.
   4. critical thinking is not really necessary in solving most everyday problems.
   5. critical thinking is demanding and time-consuming.

27. In Territory and Space, one of the two programs about Buddhism, the word "territory" is used symbolically to identify a major concept in Western thinking. It means

1.	self-interest.
2.	personal achievement.
3.	ownership.
4.	materialism.
5.	all of the above.

28.	According to Brustein the function of the professional critic is to

1.	recommend a work of art to an audience that is inexperienced in matters of artistic values.
2.	define and analyze matters of taste by absolute standards.
3.	improve people's personal taste.
4.	express his personal response to the work since standards of excellence are relative.
5.	accommodate shifts in popular opinion.

29.	Which of the following views would you express toward moral censorship of the arts?

1.	Censorship is necessary because offensive subject matter is imitated in real life.
2.	Artists should be free to ignore the bourgeois values of the moral majority.
3.	The artist's vision of truth should not be suppressed, no matter how grim it is.
4.	In order to be morally uplifting, art should depict what life ought to be like.
5.	To the pure, all things are pure.

30.	Which of the following ideas is not contained in Tolstoy's theory about art?

1.	Art must contribute toward the betterment of life.
2.	Art must appeal to ordinary people like peasants and farmers.
3.	Art must be directed toward human brotherhood.
4.	Art must be defined as what each individual finds beautiful.
5.	Art must appeal to universally held feelings.

31.	One theory of the function of art is that it should bring about a better world. Which of the following attitudes is NOT seen in the text as a problem with this concept?

1.	Universal standards of excellence would prevent second-rate artists from rising to the top.
2.	This concept would require that in all stories the protagonist would be morally improved; hence much great literature would be disqualified.
3.	Works of art too difficult for undeveloped taste would be eliminated.
4.	Esthetic sensibility would not be required of those who set standards.
5.	If critics are given power to enforce their moral standards, the fate of the artists who fail to conform would be in question.

32.	The invention of criticism is attributed to

1.	journalists.

2. Robert Brustein.
3. the Greeks.
4. Monday morning quarterbacks.
5. a negative streak in human nature.

33. A critical perspective requires that if a musical composition, for instance, seems not to fit the definition of works in the same genre, the critic ought to

1. judge it for its own worth.
2. redefine the genre.
3. condemn it for failing to meet universal standards of excellence.
4. reconsider his own criteria for that particular genre.
5. decide to what genre it properly belongs before making a decision on the work.

34. The Restoration playwright William Congreve, responding to criticism of the subject matter of his plays, said that

1. the playwright's function is to mirror his times faithfully.
2. he refused to depict vice on the stage.
3. in the interest of the moral betterment of society, his plays depicted the unhappy outcome of violence and depravity.
4. he always showed virtue triumphant.
5. the subject of a play is not important, since virtue and vice have no universal criteria.

35. George Orwell objected to the Art for Art's Sake school of criticism on the grounds that

1. it often praised a work simply because it was the product of a diseased mind.
2. it set rigid, narrow esthetic standards.
3. by accepting anti-social subject matter in the arts it encouraged anti-social behavior.
4. it rejects experimentation in form and style.
5. 1 and 3.

36. Art for Art's Sake is a school of criticism that holds the view that

1. subject matter is irrelevant to the worth of a work of art.
2. the function of art is to promote the brotherhood of man.
3. art that contains anti-social subject matter should be withheld from children.
4. the function of art is to elevate human consciousness of beauty.
5. art should advance the cause of the common man.

37. Jonathan Swift held, with most eighteenth-century critics, the view that

1. art must truthfully depict life, even the seamy side.
2. what is great art is a matter of personal definition.
3. the function of art is to bring sweetness and light to human existence.
4. critics should not be given the power to force their standards on society.
5. esthetic standards are defined differently in different cultures.

38. <u>Phoenix and Finnegan</u> recounts how the novelist James Joyce took an old drinking song about an Irish wake that became a little violent and turned it into

    1.   a savage attack on Catholicism.
    2.   a condemnation of British imperialism.
    3.   the anthem for Alcoholics Anonymous.
    4.   a sociological drama about the decline of urban Ireland.
    5.   a myth about the rise and fall of humanity.

MODULE IX

Themes in the Humanities: Myth

OVERVIEW

Mythology is more than the means by which "primitive" people explained what they could not understand. The mythmaking instinct has always been a basic psychological need for the individual and a basic cultural need for the group in order to insure its survival. We can tell a great deal about ourselves from a close look at the myths which remain important to each of us and a great deal about a given culture from its principle myth figures and symbols, such as the journey, the impossible task, and magic rituals.

LEARNING OBJECTIVES

Having completed this module, you should be able to

1) define myth as a social, ethnic, and personal phenomenon.

2) analyze the hero (or world or mono-) myth as a projection of fundamental human needs and concerns.

3) describe the component parts of the hero myth.

4) demonstrate the relationship among myths, dreams, and the unconscious.

5) analyze prominent themes and symbols found in mythology.

6) apply the American myth of "The Garden" to appropriate American values.

7) summarize the purposes behind the new space-age mythology.

8) identify the myths that appear relevant to your personal experience.

9) explain how certain myth components--such as the circle and the journey--influence the structure of many works in the humanities.

10) identify the archetypes implicit in contemporary assumptions about the environment, science, the family, the hero.

Chapter 10: "Myths"

1. Make certain you can distinguish between myth as explanation and myth as the source of archetypes.

2. Why should a study of the humanities include a consideration of mythology?

3. How has Greek Mythology had a profound effect on modern psychology? Give some examples.

4. Family life does not figure in most mythologies as it does in that of the Greeks. How does the family come through in these stories?

5. Be able to compare and contrast the uses of the Agamemnon story made by Greek mythology and Eugene O'Neill.

6. What are the universal elements of the monomyth?

7. John F. Kennedy is mentioned as a real-life monomyth hero. Why? Can you identify other modern-day men and women as monomyth heroes?

8. What symbols and themes commonly occur in myths?

9. Show how the importance of magic words in mythology relates to sexual identity.

10. What is the significance of Eden as a mythic archetype?

11. What is a mandala? What does it represent? Can you identify some forms of the mandala in contemporary society?

12. The chapter points out a number of myths that help to structure modern experience. What are they? Can any of them be harmful?

VIEWING

I. Myths: The Collective Dreams of Mankind

--"Myths and dreams are essentially indistinguishable." All myths proceed from the human unconscious, which is also the source of our dream life. There are two kinds of myths, however: The private myths (dreams) which each one of us must have to structure and make sense of individual existence, and the public myths which structure and give meaning to society and human life in general.

--Note that the visual portion of the program following the opening title depicts Stonehenge and that a "freeze" shot of Stonehenge also appears behind the opening title for each program in this series.

The designers of the course decided upon Stonehenge as an appropriate symbol of humanity's unlimited potential. Erected perhaps 4,000 years ago by an unknown group of extraordinarily precocious people for what are now thought to be scientific purposes far in advance of available technology, Stonehenge will always stand as a majestic reminder of the human need to do more than is absolutely essential for survival.

But though Stonehenge was apparently designed as a means of predicting celestial phenomena such as eclipses, its appearance so many thousands of years ago almost certainly gives it significance in the history of mythology.

--Carl Jung, the psychologist, believes that there are a number of myths which seem to exist in all cultures and which comprise what he calls the "collective unconscious" or "the collective dreams of mankind." By "dreams" we can, of course, understand "aspirations" or "ideals." But Jung and others believe that mythology arises quite literally from the dreaming process and that, even though individual dream patterns certainly exist, there are also a number of universal kinds of dream which recur from age to age and from culture to culture, all filled with symbols and images expressing the universal hopes and fears of humankind. Hence the phrase "the collective unconscious." These dreams, always imperfectly understood, occur so frequently that they find their way into traditional tales. Without realizing it, humanity has created a permanent record of its dreaming.

--Many of the themes and symbols which can be found in almost all mythology are labeled archetypes by Jung and others. An archetype is a model which makes it possible for us to explain or interpret other things. Without archetypes, each new event would be a new mystery to solve. In Jung's theory, not only myths but private dreams contain these archetypes. We inherit them by virtue of being born human, and they shape our interpretations of living even as they help to frame our expectations. Once such archetype is the mandala, which appears in the opening sequence and throughout the program. The mandala (originally a Sanskrit word meaning "magic circle") is a symbol not only of cosmic but of psychic (inner) order as well. It represents the human need to believe in totality or unity, as opposed to believing that existence is merely a series of accidents or that the human self is a discontinuous phenomenon with no internal stability.

--The journey and quest represent other universal themes or archetypes found in mythology (and indeed in our private dreams as well!). Mythmakers knew that, if life ultimately makes rounded sense (the mandala symbol), life is experienced sequentially, step by step. But surely, they thought, the sequence cannot be without direction, without purpose. Hence a basic myth plot is that of a journey undertaken by the hero either in search of some particular object (such as the Holy Grail in the Arthurian myths) or for the accomplishment of a particular task (such as Theseus's slaying of the Minotaur, which is dramatized in The Dream of the Hero). While the journey is successful in some myths, by and large the hero discovers that his prize was not worth the effort or even initiates some disaster. How do you think the mythmakers in their dreams were viewing the "journey of life"?

--A number of great literary works utilize the journey and the quest as both theme and plot structure. Note that myths always seem to influence our greatest writers, who appreciate, perhaps intuitively, the underlying psychological truth in myth. Works cited include:

<blockquote>

<u>The Odyssey</u>:   Homer's epic poem of Odysseus's (Ulysses's) ten-year voyage home following the Trojan War; written, it is believed, during the 8th century B.C.

<u>Pilgrim's Progress</u>: John Bunyan's 17th century symbolic tale of the Pilgrim's (humanity's) long and difficult journey through the temptations of this world on his way to the Heavenly City.

<u>Huckleberry Finn</u>: Mark Twain's 19th century American epic about a rebellious 14 year old's quest of unlimited freedom and journey away from the restrictions of society.

<u>Don Quixote</u>:   Miguel Cervante's 16th century novel about a maddened old man's search for the perfect woman and an ideal world.

</blockquote>

--Other common myth themes: the temptress (woman's deadly powers--mythmakers originally were men!); death and rebirth; the initiation or first encounter with the existence of evil; the fall from innocence...

--Myths continue to abound in our times. The Nazi era in Germany, for example, was a projection of the myth of racial purity and superiority. (Note that the Nazi symbol of the swastika is actually another form of mandala.)

--A key myth in the development of the United Sates was that of The Garden. Europeans saw the New World as a chance to return to Eden, to lost innocence, to start anew without the accumulated sins of the human past.

--Space has become the new frontier and probably the most abundant source of new myths. It is suggested that the widespread belief in flying saucers, for example, represents people's undying need for the myth of the unknown, of un-explored possibilities, of <u>something</u> different from the humdrum reality of the workaday world.

--The fascination with other planets (the popularity of <u>Star Trek</u>, <u>Star Wars</u>, and other science fiction epics) may stem from the belief that humanity has a predestined role to play in the universe. The psychiatrist Alan McGlasham observes that for the average person space exploration is the new myth journey, as mankind now engages in a search for a new kind of Grail--the discovery of life elsewhere in the universe.

--Note that the spaceman, the new mythic hero, is enclosed, as the film ends, in yet another mandala. What statement about the space program and its purposes may underlie the recurrence of this symbol?

II. <u>Myths, The Dream of the Hero</u>

--The unconscious is that aspect of the self which does not communicate directly to our conscious, waking being. Instead, it uses the images, situations, and symbols which are found in dreams. The dreams which humanity shares in turn represent the foundations of mythology. Remember: dreams are private myths; myths, public dreams.

--The hero myth functions as a force in both the individual and the group. The individual needs heroes as models of growth, to help him discover and assert his personality. Society needs heroes to help establish its collective identity, to bring unity, a sense of order and purpose, a sense of direction. A vigorous society is one with powerful, well-defined hero myths; a weak society, one whose hero myths have lost their force. A society without such myths is, as the historian Arnold Toynbee points out, already dead.

--Viewed psychologically, the plot of the monomyth is a blueprint for individual growth. Its events portray the stages of an individual's life: the mystery of the birth-journey from timelessness into the temporal world, the dawn of self-awareness, the discovery of identity, the struggle for psychological and physical integration, the ascent of reason, the assumption of maturity, the recognition of fallibility and mortality, and the acceptance of death.

--Western civilization has continuously looked to Greece for many of its models: in art, in philosophy, in democratic government, in the achievement of the fully-rounded human being and most assuredly in mythology. And no myth of the Greeks embodies more vividly the ideals of humans than the myth of Theseus. No myth lends itself more readily to psychological interpretation. Theseus was the semimythical founder of the city of Athens, itself the acknowledged model for the rest of Greece. Theseus began his career by imitating the violent deeds of his cousin Hercules, deeds of brawn, not reason. Soon, however, he learned to master his animal aspect, symbolized by his slaying of the Minotaur in the labyrinth of his own psyche. After that, he grew in maturity as the organizer of the Athenian state, as lawmaker, as cultural hero. He set the tone and established the spirit of a nation. Then, by descending pridefully into Hades (his passions) he came to understand that even heroes are mortal, are only men. He was misunderstood, driven into exile, but ultimately took his rightful place of honor in the history of Athens. As myth hero, Theseus--not perfect, not immortal, not a god, but a complex human being--became the model for a democratic Athens. But the Athenian ideal--the human being who unifies all of the sometimes conflicting aspects of his psyche--has itself become a model for all of us as well. Other myths may offer heroes of physical and moral perfection, but surely none may be closer to the heart of what humanity is really all about; a puzzling combination of traits that in our fondest dreams add up to something after all.

THE MONOMYTH

From an astonishing number of myths there has emerged a common pattern. Indeed this well-nigh universal correspondence is thought to be the parent-stuff of a great many major myths and has been called the monomyth (the one myth that fits us all), the world myth (because of its universality), and the hero myth (because in the hero's journey of self-discovery lies the fundamental human search for meaning in life).

The monomyth is the plot also of a thousand fairy tales, legends, ballads, and folktales; and the substructure of innumerable works of civilized art: operas, plays, novels, short stories, films, and TV dramas.

The specific plot of the monomyth may vary from time to time and place to place, but the pattern is very much the same. According to Lord Raglan, a prominent mythologist of our day, a typical version might run something like this:

1. The hero's mother is a royal virgin.

2. His father is a king, and

3. Often a near relative of his mother, but

4. The circumstances of his conception are unusual, and

5. He is also reputed to be the son of a god.

6. At birth an attempt is made, usually by his father or his maternal grandfather to kill him, but

7. He is spirited away, and

8. Reared by foster-parents in a far country.

9. We are told nothing of his childhood, but

10. On reaching manhood he returns or goes to his future kingdom.

11. After a victory over the king and/or giant, dragon, or wild beast,

12. He marries a princess, often the daughter of his predecessor, and

13. Becomes a king.

14. For a time he reigns uneventfully, and

15. Prescribes laws, but

16. Later, he loses favor with the gods, and/or his subjects, and

17. Is driven from the throne and city, after which

18. He meets with a mysterious death,

19. Often at the top of a hill.

20. His children, if any, do not succeed him.

21. His body is not buried, but nevertheless

22. He has one or more holy sepulchres.

According to Lord Raglan, on a scale of these twenty-two points, Oedipus scores twenty-one; Theseus, twenty; Romulus, eighteen; Hercules, seventeen; Perseus, eighteen; Jason, fifteen; Siegfried, eleven: king Arthur, nineteen; and Robin Hood, thirteen; and Jewish, Japanese, African, and Celtic heroes make scores ranging from nine to eighteen. We have here, accordingly, not merely a catalog of heroic traits but an archetypal plot, a motif of circumstances so frequently encountered that it becomes coextensive with heroic story and drama.

How would a modern hero measure against the Raglan scale? Marshall Fishwick, in his book The Hero: American Style, selects the most recent heroic American President, John F. Kennedy, to demonstrate how modern examples may continue to fit the ancient mold:

> His father was called to royal court (as Ambassador to the court of Saint James) and the son was educated by (presumably) wise men (at Harvard). Then he went off to fight an evil dragon (the Japanese Navy) and after a bloody fracas (PT 109) triumphed and returned to marry the beautiful princess (Jackie). Having inherited his father's kingdom (politics), he fought and defeated a second contender (Nixon) before taking over as ruler (President). For a time he reigned smoothly and prescribed laws. Then he suddenly lost favor (Bay of Pigs), tried to rally his people, and died a sudden and mysterious death (Did Oswald really shoot Kennedy?). Amid great mourning (the first worldwide televised funeral) he was buried on a sacred hillside (Arlington). Now he has many shrines (a cultural center, airport, library, highway, and space launching site.)

SELF-TEST

Match each item in the first column with an item in the second. Use no item more than one time.

VT	1.	Theseus	opposed to civilization		_____
VT	2.	monomyth	related to way psychic life is organized		_____
VT	3.	mandala			
VT	4.	archetypes	mythological vision of United States		_____
T	5.	Oedipus	models for actions and thoughts		_____
V	6.	John F. Kennedy	his life meets requirements of world myth		_____
V	7.	Stonehenge			
VT	8.	Carl Jung	theory of the collective unconscious		_____
T	9.	The Garden	myth figure of interest to Freud		_____
T	10.	new mythological frontier	symbol of humanistic needs		_____
T	11.	primitivism	found in all ages and cultures		_____
			space		_____

CHECK LIST OF MAIN IDEAS

1. Both dreams and myths arise from the unconscious, and represent our aspirations, fantasies, and fears. The events in each are symbolic and represent ways in which an individual or a culture organizes or responds to experience.

2. Some myths represent early explanations for natural phenomena, and so constitute a pre-scientific view of the world. But a good deal of mythology can be considered profoundly true in the sense that it reflects the nature of existence as it seems to human beings.

3. A great deal of uniformity occurs in mythic themes and symbols throughout all cultures (e.g., the journey, mandala).

4. One universal or archetypal myth, the monomyth, is a tale occurring throughout the world and the ages.

5. The hero of the monomyth fits a common pattern: circumstances of his birth are unusual, he goes on a journey during which he performs a heroic act, generally with catastrophic consequences; he loses favor with the gods or his people, and later meets a mysterious death, often on a hilltop.

6. Myth archetypes continue to influence modern attitudes toward matters of universal concerns.

MYTHS AND THE HUMAN QUINTESSENCE

by

Donald M. Early

WHAT IS MYTH?

Much confusion surrounds the word myth. In the popular mind, myth connotes something false, not fact, the opposite of reality. . . as in such expressions as "The myth of political equality," "The power shortage: Myth or reality?"

Myth also means an exotic tale or story from the past, usually associated with religion, and hence peopled with gods, heroes, and legendary creatures, all actors in a superhuman drama.

To serious minds, myth signifies, and has always signified in all cultures and in all times something far deeper, something that lies close to the central meaning of life and that can only be indirectly expressed, in the form of a story or a metaphor. Myth at this level is seen as a kind of net in which is captured the profound, elusive essence of what it is to be human.

Virtually all scholars--the anthropologists, psychologists, mythologists, philosophers, poets, and so on--assume this view of myth in their definitions. Let us look at some of the ways they define myth.

"Myths are the instruments by which we continually struggle to make our experience intelligible to ourselves. A myth is a large, controlling image that gives philosophical meaning to the facts of ordinary life: that is, which has organizing value for experience. ...Myth is the essential substructure of all human activity."

-- Mark Schorer

"Myth is a complex of stories, some no doubt fact, and some fantasy, which, for various reasons human beings regard as demonstrations of the inner meaning of the universe and of human life."

-- Alan Watts

"Myth is a condensed account of man's being and attempts to represent reality with structural fidelity, to indicate at a single stroke the salient and fundamental relations which for man constitute reality. Myth is not an obscure, oblique or elaborate way of expressing reality; it is the ONLY way."

-- George Whalley

Let us consider that last statement in Whalley's definition: "The ONLY way... of expressing reality." All of reality? That seems a large order for myth or any other system of representation to fill. But IS there any other way for us to tell our story, the whole of it?

Suppose one day a creature from outer space were to visit us, and ask, "What is it like to be a human being?" What would we answer? How would we begin? By showing him (we'll call the visitor "him") our marvelous accomplishments in science, our great cities, our libraries? (Surely all these would seem quite primitive to him!). By taking him to a maternity ward, a nursery, a school, a factory, the U.N. headquarters, a cemetery? Would that make him understand? Would it tell him what it means to be a certain kind of creature who has evolved over millions of years in a certain kind of planetary environment, and who carries in his body and impressed in his brain the living evidence of his long, upward journey?

Even if we assume we could impart all that, would there not be something still missing from our account? Some mystery that we feel surrounds our existence, and relates to our destiny in the cosmos? Instinct and experience alike tell us that the whole of life is greater than the sum of its parts. Therefore, what would be missing from our account would be the essence of our humanness--or rather what the Greeks called "quintessence," meaning that indefinable fifth element still present in phenomena after all else has been accounted for by the four basic elements of creation: earth, air, fire, and water.

Where, however, shall we find the quintessence of human life? For that is what our space visitor is really asking for. Ultimately, we shall have to fall back on our myths. For it seems they alone have the capacity to contain quintessence. Myths alone can present the whole of our complex paradoxical condition "in a single stroke"...as metaphor, as a story that resembles a dream.

THE POWER OF MYTHS

Myths have their basis in dreams. Both myths and dreams speak the same symbolic language; both serve the same purpose: to keep all areas of our psychic life, conscious and unconscious, in touch with one another, to keep us aware of the totality of being.

Our dreams as individuals constitute our private myths. Our dream experiences provide the mythic and heroic elements so often lacking in everyday life, and so necessary to nourish spirit and to reaffirm our invisible dimension.

But we humans also dream in common, we are told. Psychologists and anthropologists have noted that in the dreams of individuals everywhere, in every race and culture, are many recurrent patterns and figures and motifs clearly pointing to a common reservoir of dream material. This reservoir the psychologist Carl G. Jung calls the "collective unconscious," meaning by that the portion of our psychic life believed to be inherited--i.e. not that contributed by personal experience. It

135

consists in part of innumerable innate patterns of behavior, by means of which we are able to respond to experience. Such patterns Jung calls <u>archetypes</u>, a word that means "first models." Archetypes provide the "models" for action, for thought, and for structuring the growth process in individuals and groups.

Although archetypes appear to influence every aspect of our existence, they find their most comprehensive expression in the body of world myths. Here the most common archetypal motifs are such figures as the Hero, the Scapegoat, the Outcast, the Monster-Slayers, the Star-Crossed Lovers, the Devil, and the Woman Figure in a variety of aspects: Earthmother, Temptress, Platonic Ideal, and Unfaithful Wife.

Common archetypal situations in myths include the Quest, the Descent to the Underworld, the Task, the Sacrifice, the Loss of the Innocent Paradise, the Flood, the Virgin Birth, the Land of the Dead, the Return, and many, many more.

Appearing also are many archetypal configurations, such as the Flower, the Jewel (especially the diamond and pearl), the Egg, the Golden Ball (or Apple), the Chalice (or Grail)...and, most prominently, those concentric radial arrangements that we call mandalas. Mandalas are among the oldest forms of human expression, found painted on the walls of paleolithic caves, and engraved on ancient artifacts. Mandalas have innumerable variations, the most common of which are the rayed circle or sunwheel, the swastika, the cross, the circle or square with a central point, and so on. According to scholars, mandalas seem in some yet indecipherable way related to the basic organization of psychic life, possibly of all life and--if we may believe the microphysicists--of all matter, too.

Myths, through their archetypal contents, mirror the nature and meaning of human existence. They embody the universally shared hopes and fears and preoccupations of mankind. Jung calls myths "the collective dreams of mankind."

Hence, far from presenting "what is false, not fact, the opposite of reality"...myths embody the profoundest human truths. They are, as one modern sage has expressed it, "the nearest approach to <u>absolute</u> truth that can be stated in words."

YESTERDAY AND TODAY

In the past, in traditional societies, according to Joseph Campbell, the mythological system of a people or a culture functioned in four ways. It served to link "regular waking consciousness with the vast mystery and wonder of the universe." It presented "some intelligible image or picture of nature"; validated and enforced "a specific social and moral order"; and finally provided "a marked pathway to carry the individual through the stages of life."

In contemporary society, however, it is apparent that myths no longer function in so pervasive and comprehensive a manner. The great controlling myths of Western civilization--Christianity, capitalism, the belief in man as the measure of all things, and the belief in the omniscience of science, in individual liberty, in progress--have suffered serious erosion, and in many areas of modern life have been discredited. The social fabric, once thought cohesive, has become fragmented and--what is worse--severed from its unconscious roots.

Inevitably, when the social structuring force of the unconscious is dissolved, the individual is thrown back upon himself. Since life without myth is intolerable for him, he is forced to become his own myth-maker. He is compelled to undertake his own psychological, inward journey in search of new forms and renewed mythic content.

MYTH IN THE MODERN WORLD

So archetypal is the need for heroes that the hero plot seems almost a reflexive response to certain life experiences. If our everyday world seems somewhat lacking in monomythic hero-types, our fantasy world continues to spawn them all about us. Perhaps nowhere is this myth-making process more at work than in the world of advertising. Here each day, in the magical country of Consumer-land, innumerable mini-myths act out the heroic scenario.

*A damsel in distress is battling the presence of evil in one of its many guises: odors, pain, a dissatisfied husband, spotted dishes, or any of the hundreds of life situations that pass as tragedy in the world. The mythic hero can be a real character or the product itself come to life. The product solves the problem in an instant, transforms the distressed damsel back into a princess and, the commercial implies, the happy ending means that the housewife is herself a hero of sorts, an alchemist who turns dirty floors, dishes and clothes into shiny new ones with the aid of her solutions. To the degree that they are successful, these commercials turn housework into a task with mythic dimensions.

Far from being mere fancy, these mythological parallels find a real-life, flesh-and-blood embodiment in a new type of hero who nevertheless continues to fit the classic mold, one who might have walked right out of the world of Arthurian legend. For like King Arthur, Ralph Nader believes that a better, purer world is possible once the land has been cleansed of its oppressors, villains, and evil monsters. "We aren't coming to the end of the Dark Age," he says. "We're in the middle of it." So, he gathers about him his own round table of crusading knights, known as Nader's Raiders, and together they pit themselves against the villains of shoddy consumer products, the adulterers of foods and drinks, the industrial ogres who turn out automobiles that are deathtraps, the factory monsters that foul the air and streams of our land. One by one the giants are toppled or worsted in combat; the evils are exposed; the grateful consumer is rescued. Though his enemies never cease to plot against him, Sir Ralph rides on in his blameless, ascetic way, never once losing sight of the Grail, or failing to give his all to the cause...the universal marks of the true hero.

*Jeffrey Schrank. "Mythology Today" in Media & Methods, April, 1973

About Myths

Bruno Bettelheim. <u>The Uses of Enchantment</u> (New York: Alfred A. Knopf, 1976). An eminent child psychologist looks into Freudian and other meanings and significance in fairy tales.

Joseph Campbell. <u>The Hero with a Thousand Faces</u> (New York: Bollingen Foundation, 1961). A scholarly and profoundly psychological study of the monomyth and its many revelations about ourselves.

_____. <u>Myths to Live By</u> (New York: The Viking Press, 1972). A discussion of how particular myths continue to reflect human needs.

Lord Raglan. <u>The Hero: A Study in Tradition, Myth, and Drama</u> (New York: Vintage Books, 1956). This highly readable book analyzes the nature of the hero myth or monomyth and the psychological and social needs it fills. It also contains a full discussion of the myth's universality and how it illuminates what we are really like.

Myths Themselves

Unless otherwise noted, all of the following are available in various editions and translations.

General: <u>The Age of Fable</u> by Thomas Bulfinch. (New York: Crowell, 1970). This readable retelling of the myths in simple fictional form has introduced generations of readers to legendary heroes from several different cultures. Ulysses, Beowulf, King Arthur, Cupid, and Robin Hood are among the characters to be found here.

____: <u>Mythology</u> by Edith Hamilton. (Boston: Little Brown, 1942). A definitive collection and lucid presentation of Greek, Roman, and Norse mythologies by an eminent classical scholar.

Babylon: <u>Gilgamesh</u>. (See Recommended Reading, Module IV).

England: <u>The Once and Future King</u> by T. H. White. (New York: G. P. Putnam's Sons, 1958). An account of Medieval England and King Arthur's Court that combines history and myth in a unique work.

Germany: <u>The Nibelungenlied</u>. A long series of both heroic and tragic deeds all related to the struggle for possession of a magic ring which makes its owner master of the universe.

Greece: <u>The Iliad of Homer</u> (See Recommended Reading, Module IV)

<u>The Odyssey of Homer</u> (See Viewing, this chapter)

India: <u>The Bhagavad-Gita</u> (See Recommended Reading, Module VII)

Mexico: The Teachings of Don Juan, A Yaqui Way of Knowledge by Carlos Castenada. (Berkeley: University of California Press, 1967). The story of a young man's journey into the hallucinatory world of drugs under the tutelage of a Yaqui Indian with remarkable powers.

"Middle-Earth": The Lord of the Rings by J.R.R. Tolkien (Boston: Houghton-Mifflin, 1966). A story of high adventure in a world inhabited by many fantastic beings including Frodo the hobbit, the unwitting possessor of a magic ring which corrupts all who wear it.

Rome: The Aeneid of Virgil. Aeneas's journey from fallen Troy to Italy, where he is said to have founded the Roman Empire.

MODULE X

Themes in the Humanities: Love

OVERVIEW

Love is a concept surviving through history, though radically altering its meaning and significance from time to time and from culture to culture. Love is both an experience not universally understood or shared and a romantic ideal widespread in our culture. Hence a choice among definitions of love is possible. Certainly the range of possibilities is at least as great as it seemed to the Greeks, who placed eros, or physical love, at one end of the spectrum and agapé, or spiritual love, at the other. The amount of unhappiness suffered in the name of love suggests that very often people's expectations about love do not match reality.

LEARNING OBJECTIVES

Having completed this module, you should be able to

1) summarize some of the major definitions of love relative to particular times and cultures.

2) distinguish among various types of love relationships, such as familial love, friendship, and altruism.

3) compare and contrast theories of love advanced by Plato, St. Paul, La Rochefoucauld, Freud, and Fromm.

4) trace the derivation and continuing impact of romantic love as an ideal.

5) point out examples of the persistence of the Victorian model of male/female relationships.

6) show how traditional attitudes toward "masculine" and "feminine" spring from historical and cultural contexts as much as the ideals of love relationships.

7) point out the characteristics of Ibsen's A Doll's House which stamp the play as a pioneer work in liberation literature.

Chapter 11: "Love"

1. Romantic love was not a concept apparent in classical mythology and literature. Analyze the attitudes that did prevail toward love among the ancient Greeks and Romans.

2. Describe the family model that developed in ancient Hebrew communities, and be able to show a correspondence between the development of their religious ideas and their concept of family roles.

3. Platonic love is often mistakenly considered to be a nonsexual relationship. Sex can exist in Platonic love. Therefore, what is Platonic love, really?

4. To what source is romantic love traced in the text? Do you consider romantic love to be still prominent as an ideal today?

5. How did the convention of courtly love raise the status of women in the Middle Ages?

6. What is meant by the "Victorian model"? Model of what? Is it still around?

7. Be able to trace changing attitudes toward love, marriage, and sex roles in the decades since the 40s.

8. There seems to be evidence of a return to traditional family values in our society. What evidence is cited in the text? Do you agree with the conclusion drawn from this evidence?

9. The suggestion is made that in the contemporary world conditions call for a different perception of the roles of men and women. Do you agree that the rules of love are more complicated and varied now than ever before?

10. Does the chapter conclude with an optimistic or a pessimistic view of modern love? Or is it neutral on the subject?

VIEWING

I. Love: Myth and Mystery

   --The narrator is a celebrated author writing a book called Love: Myth and Mystery. It becomes increasingly clear that his concern for the subject has been motivated by a relationship with the young lady in the photograph. The exact nature of this relationship is never to be made precisely clear, and we are left to wonder whether the narrator/hero will ever fully understand it either. But perhaps ambiguity is the point of the film.

--The first view of love that goes through the hero's mind is embodied in the true
   story of Peter Abelard, a medieval monk and philosopher, and Eloise, a girl he
   once married in secret, only to be separated from her by an angry family. Both
   later consecrated their lives to God, but many have wondered whether the love of
   God was not a spiritualization of sexual attraction.

--Though he attempts to remain objective in his review of love's history, the hero
   suggests by his mannerisms a definite preference for one type of love. Can you
   tell which?

--The Greeks developed a belief in two contrasting love experiences. One was
   eros, or the sensual, physical celebration of love. The other was agapé, or a
   nonphysical relationship best described as a meeting of souls. The Greek ideal
   was to maintain balance between the two.

--The Platonic theory of love starts in eros and proceeds to agapé. Plato
   accepted physical love as a joyous experience, but felt it was only the first
   step in a relationship that eventually became the sharing of ideas and universal
   knowledge. In the popular mind Platonic love signifies the nonsexual period in
   a relationship, but this is an inaccurate simplification.

--The section on the Hebrew Bible focuses on Hebrew family and tribal loyalties in
   which the interest of the group is always more important than that of the
   individual. Some have attributed to the Hebrews the ideal of loyalty to one's
   family.

--The section on Christianity stresses two things. One is altruistic love as
   embodied in the teachings of Jesus. The other is the dramatic separation which
   St. Paul made between the lower or animal self and the higher or spiritual self.
   For Paul, as for many later Christians, eros remained a debased version of love.
   For St. Jerome the sinfulness of the flesh even tainted the marriage
   relationship.

--Medieval "romances" are stories and poems usually centering on an idealized love
   that exists outside the institution of marriage. In the Middle Ages and early
   Renaissance the basis for marriage, at least among the upper classes, was
   generally money or property. Love was usually found elsewhere, but, since in
   those Christian times sexual encounters outside of marriage were of course
   sinful, the authors of the romances are singularly vague about the extent of
   intimacy, the implication always being present that something like "spiritual
   intimacy" was the true bond. In any event, "romantic" (from the French for
   "narrative tale") love continues to suggest a relationship in which physical
   intimacy is not the sole reason for an attachment.

--The advent of Freudian psychology was disastrous to the literature of romantic
   love, which had survived for many centuries. Serious writers began to give
   their characters an "unconscious" and/or an "id" to describe relationships
   between the sexes, with increasing frankness, in terms of unconscious "drives"
   or the "libido."

--A contemporary anti-Freudian approach to love is that of Erich Fromm, who finds
   that people seek each other because they fear separateness. For Fromm, it is
   immature to desire another solely out of psychological need. Really strong

143

relationships exist between people who do not need each other but are able to enrich each other's life through their mutual strength.

--The hero's final attitude is not Fromm or Freud or Plato. Instead, he quotes some lines from a poem by Archibald MacLeish ("Not Marble nor the Gilded Monuments"). The lines appear to be somewhat detached, but there is more behind "I will say the shape of a leaf lay once on your hair" than just those simple words, isn't there?

II. Roles We Play

--Reference is made to the role of women in Greek society. Often the most liberated and intellectual women were "professionals" who served as hostesses in private establishments to which men came not only for sensual pleasure but intellectual conversation. As if aware of the competition from these women, the poet Sappho opened a school at which aspiring wives were taught the subtle arts of "entertaining" their husbands.

--Mariolatry, or the cult of the Virgin, was a literary, artistic, and religious phenomenon of the Middle Ages, one which enhanced the position of women in Western society. The adoration of the Virgin, expressed in poetry, painting, sculpture, and architecture, evolved into a profound sense of male subservience to women, especially virgins. This cult led eventually to the chivalric code and the relationship between gallant knight and lady fair.

--The Victorian lady who has just seen "Mr. Ibsen's play" was affected by A Doll's House (1879)--a play that shocked its audiences by questioning the double standard, whereby men could with impunity do things that women could not do at all. Ibsen's heroine walks out on her husband, but she must face a society unprepared for her liberation. Is society ready yet?

--The main part of the program deals with three examples of male-female relationships in today's society. Nora and David probably represent the liberated-chic couple mentioned in the text chapter.

--Claire believes that motherhood is the proper destiny for a woman and a responsibility she owes to her husband, who "proves" himself to society by fathering children. Claire obviously is feeling a sense that, in mothering four children to the exclusion of any other self-concern, she has perhaps missed out on her development as a human being.

--Both Tom and David reflect the importance of the macho image in our society. It is not clear whether Tom and David in their zeal for physical fitness are driven by the need to impress themselves, each other, society, or their wives, who certainly give no indication that they desire such Spartan discipline from their mates.

--The third "couple" is of course only half represented. Dennis has long since disappeared. Gail's problem is probably less loneliness than the fact that in this small town there is no approved role for a divorcee or a middle-aged unattached woman.

--At the reunion the women seem to be lapsing into very traditional and time-honored sex role stereotypes. One might ask oneself whether the reason is

144

that these roles really work, hence are desirable, or that each woman feels the need to pretend that such is the case. If so, who began the pretense? Why could there not have been total honesty from the beginning?

--We are not told how Tom, Claire, and Gail will live out their lives. David and Nora, however, indicate that they have learned an important lesson from the reunion and propose to make profound changes in their lives. What do you think these might be? Do you think they will work?

SELF-TEST

Match each item in the first column with an item in the second. Use no item more than one time.

T	1.	altruism	eros leads to agapé	_____
VT	2.	Platonic love	veneration of the Virgin in medieval Christianity	_____
T	3.	romantic love		
V	4.	Victorian model	a code produced within medieval aristocracy	_____
V	5.	Erich Fromm	underlies many current attitudes toward sex roles	_____
V	6.	Abelard		
V	7.	Gail's problem	unable to handle role reversal in "liberated" marriage	_____
V	8.	David's problem	love for another more than for oneself	_____
T	9.	Mariolatry		
T	10.	chivalry	guilt because of divorce and lack of children	_____
T	11.	The Courtier	developed a model for family life	_____
T	12.	Lady Chatterly's Lover	attacks Victorian repressiveness	_____
T	13.	Judaism	warns against loving out of a sense of dependency	_____
T	14.	The Way of the World		
			began in the Middle Ages, still with us as an ideal	_____
			sophisticated, practical instruction in conduct of love affairs	_____
			depicts liberalized role of women in the Restoration period	_____
			famous martyr in the history of love	_____

CHECK LIST OF MAIN IDEAS

1. Love takes many forms, with varying levels of honesty and profundity.

2. Only those who possess a strong feeling of self-worth can love others honestly and deeply. Feelings of inadequacy prevent individuals from opening up, as well as causing them to seek to achieve self-importance at the expense of others.

3. Customs and environment, as well as personal inadequacy, often provide barriers to one's ability to express and to be comfortable with feelings of genuine affection.

4. We are living at a time when many are recommending the elimination of old-fashioned, outmoded sex-role stereotypes, yet these persist more than we realize. Even when people openly endorse the creed of liberation, however, some are likely to be changing the way they talk, not the way they behave.

RECOMMENDED READING

Simone de Beauvoir. <u>The Second Sex</u> (New York: Alfred A. Knopt, 1953). One of the first examinations of the role of modern women by a noted existentialist.

Marilyn French. <u>The Women's Room</u> (New York: Jove Publications, Inc., 1977). A popular novel which chronicles the development of contemporary female sensibility from traditional marriage and motherhood through divorce, to a radical change in her self-image and attitude towards a woman's options in life.

Erich Fromm. <u>The Art of Loving</u> (New York: Harper, 1956). A detailed examination of various kinds of relationships which can be called "love," with an emphasis on the author's recommended definition of love as mutual enhancement of two strong lives.

Jan de Hartog. "The Four Poster" in <u>Best American Plays, 4th Series</u> ed. John Gassner (New York: Crown, 1958). The dramatic chronicle of a marriage set entirely in a bedroom, reflecting many of the sex roles of the past fifty years.

Morton Hunt. <u>The Natural History of Love</u> (New York: Minerva Press, 1959). A readable and witty social history in which the author shows that there has been no universal view or practice of love throughout Western culture.

Henrik Ibsen. "A Doll's House" in <u>Eleven Plays by Henrik Ibsen</u> (New York: Modern Library). Perhaps the first play in the history of theater in which a wife, refusing to define herself through her husband's value system, decides to leave him.

Plato. <u>Symposium</u> tr. B. Jowett (New York: Classics Club, 1942). This is the dialog which contains Plato's theory of love.

Alexander Pope. "Eloisa to Abelard" in <u>The Poems of Alexander Pope</u> ed. John Butt (New Haven: Yale University Press, 1963). Pope's most serious poem, in which Eloise addresses her former love, now a monk, and confesses that despite her own spiritual dedication to the veil, she is not yet free of passion.

William Shakespeare. <u>Romeo and Juliet</u> and <u>Taming of the Shrew</u> (both appear in various editions). A most interesting double feature enabling the reader to contrast the romanticism of the youthful Shakespeare with what could be the sexism of the playwright's maturity.

Leo Tolstoy. <u>Anna Karenina</u> tr. Louise and Aylmer Maude. (London: Oxford University Press, 1961). The classic story of a tragedy which befalls a woman who dares to defy the standards of her society.

1. Lawrence's <u>Lady Chatterley's Lover</u> was an extremely controversial novel in its time. Many condemned it as pornography, but in reality it revolves around which serious theme?

   1. a criticism of Victorian repressiveness
   2. a denial of class barriers
   3. the undeniable, if tragic, need to retain the class system
   4. an altered view of suicide
   5. a realistic depiction of British exploitation

2. Which of the following views of love delineated in <u>Love: Myth and Mystery</u> struck you as being the most cynical? That of

   1. St. Paul.
   2. Freud.
   3. romantic love.
   4. Eloise and Abelard.
   5. I found none of them cynical.

3. In Plato's <u>Symposium</u>, his major dialog on the subject of love, the philosopher presents the view that human beings go through a variety of "loves" in ascending order, finally achieving a highly abstract and intellectual form of love. Of the following, which kind of love does Plato consider the least fulfilling?

   1. eros
   2. agapé
   3. symbiosis
   4. entelechy
   5. dialectic

4. Which of the following terms is the one used by Carl Jung as a label for the characters, events and symbols in myths? It is a synonym for "universal mode."

   1. theme
   2. stereotype
   3. archetype
   4. Form
   5. none of the above

5. The Study Guide points out that the life of John F. Kennedy meets nearly all of the requirements of something. What is it?

    1. the points on a mandala
    2. monomyth
    3. a tragedy
    4. an epic poem
    5. an ancient prophecy

6. The program The Collective Dreams of Mankind indicated that the rise to international prominence of America during the nineteenth century led to a revival of one of humanity's oldest and most durable myths. This can be called the myth of the

    1. ocean.
    2. garden.
    3. mountain.
    4. temptress.
    5. cowboy.

7. Platonic love is sometimes mistakenly thought of as a totally nonsexual relationship. Plato did not advise against physical love, but the love which bears his name must have an element which is usually missing from a purely physical relationship. This element is

    1. a meeting of minds.
    2. the clear dominance of one over the other.
    3. mutual passivity.
    4. mutual transcendentalism.
    5. conformity to moral standards.

8. The program Love: Myth and Mystery dealt with the fate of a person named Abelard. Who was he?

    1. a philosopher of the 12th century
    2. a French doctor
    3. a mid-Western schoolteacher
    4. a novelist writing a book on love
    5. a psychologist who dispelled the myth of love

9. Which of the following BEST states the point of the ballet in Love: Myth and Mystery depicting the love of the blind young man for the ugly girl?

    1. True love is of the soul not the body.
    2. Medieval marriages were economical and social arrangements.
    3. In love it is intellectual compatibility that matters most.
    4. "Ugly" and "beautiful" are relative terms and are defined by social convention.
    5. Physical attractiveness very often is the determining factor in a love relationship.

10. The program Roles We Play implies that in every human relationship the participants play one part or another, sometimes changing parts unexpectedly. What overall statement about human roles is being made by this program?

1. that everyone is basically a hypocrite when it comes to role-playing
2. that the basic role we play is that of energetic youth
3. that suppressed sexuality is at the root of all relationships
4. that one must choose those roles which feel most comfortable
5. that the family has become an outmoded institution in this rapidly changing world

11. Which of the following observations on myths is most accurate and defensible?

1. They are no longer relevant in our age.
2 Early people avoided myths since thinking was not well-developed.
3. Myths developed from the need to explain creation, humanity, and death.
4. Humans long ago outgrew the need for mythology.
5. Myths offer people a fantasy refuge from unhappy realities.

12. Greek mythology could stand on its own merits as literature, but it has proved invaluable also as a source of insight into

1. contemporary physics.
2. archetypes of state structures.
3. the origins of human language.
4. the ideal educational model.
5. motives behind human behavior.

13. Which of the following observations comes closest to expressing the TRUE function of mythology in human culture?

1. Its sole reason for existing is to explain the unknown before scientific evidence is available.
2. It makes people feel that they are of little importance in the universe.
3. It creates models by which we may organize our understanding of ourselves and our universe.
4. It makes possible a continuing belief in life beyond the grave.
5. It reinforces an optimistic faith in the human potential, without which we should perish.

24. All of the following elements tend to appear in world myths EXCEPT one. Which is it?

1. The hero is supposedly descended from a god.
2. The hero conquers a wild beast.
3. The hero loses favor with the gods or his people.
4. The hero's death is mysterious.
5. The hero is reunited with his lost love just before his death.

15. The tradition of romantic love originated during

1. the Victorian Age.
2. the silent film era.
3. the Middle Ages.
4. the early days of the radio soap operas.
5. the final years of the Roman Empire.

16. In his play, A Doll's house, Henrik Ibsen shocked audiences of the late 19th and early 20th centuries by suggesting that

    1. a woman should not sacrifice her individuality for a marriage.
    2. parents should use birth control and limit family size to three children.
    3. a husband's honor should be saved at the expense of his wife's if necessary.
    4. women should use the power of the ballot to change the political system.
    5. in reality the male image was defined and limited by the female.

17. In early Hebraic times one kind of earthly love was stressed above all others. It was the love of

    1. husband and wife.
    2. the beautiful things of this world created by God.
    3. self, which must come before love of others.
    4. family and tribe.
    5. power, without which society was not possible.

18. If a wife accuses a husband of being "Victorian" in his outlook and action--as the term is used in this module--she probably means that he is

    1. prudish and easily shocked by his children's behavior.
    2. convinced that her place is in the home.
    3. extremely fussy about neatness and order.
    4. inhibited in expressing sexual passion.
    5. all of the above.

19. The program Love: Myth and Mystery dealt with the fate of the person named Abelard. Who was he?

    1. a philosopher of the 12th century
    2. a French doctor
    3. a mid-Western school teacher
    4. a novelist writing a book on love
    5. a psychologist who dispelled the myth of love

20. La Rochefoucauld said: "There are people who would never be in love if they had never heard of love." Which of the following represents the best restatement of what the philosopher meant?

    1. Love is a cultural and social phenomenon, not a basic instinct or need.
    2. In matters of love people are fickle.
    3. It doesn't take much to persuade people they are in love.
    4. Romantic fiction ought to tell the truth about love.
    5. none of the above.

21. Roles We Play is a program about the way in which certain definitions of male and female, imposed upon us from external sources, affect our relationships both with the opposite sex and ourselves. Which character in your estimation had the LEAST understanding of himself/herself?

    1. Nora, because she really wanted to be a wife and mother

151

2. David, because he really wanted to be the breadwinner of the family
3. Gail, because she really wanted to look young and sexy
4. Claire, because she really wanted to be like Nora
5. Tom, because he really wanted a mother, not a wife

22. The theories and discoveries of Sigmund Freud had an enormous impact in many areas of human thought and expression. The ideal of romantic love was especially hard hit because of Freud's contention that

1. people seek their exact duplicates in love partners.
2. people are secretly looking for parent substitutes when they fall in love.
3. people seek their exact opposites in love partners.
4. people are only looking for financial security when they fall in love.
5. people only fall in love to escape from family rules and regulations.

23. The Greeks made a distinction between love of the body and love of the spirit, but they did not say that the former was to be avoided. To which of the following can we trace the idea that physical love, except among married people is sinful and appalling?

1. St. Teresa
2. St. Luke
3. St. Paul
4. the medieval cult of the Virgin
5. Freud

24. The Collective Dreams of Mankind concludes with an analysis of the predominant form of contemporary mythology. According to this analysis, which of the following figures would you be most likely to find in a modern myth?

1. a private detective
2. a dropout
3. a spaceman
4. a soldier of fortune
5. the self-made executive

25. Donald Early's essay in Module IX of the Study Guide indicates that, if we had to explain what human beings are to a visitor from space, we would most likely use which of the following as our illustration?

1. myths
2. a painting of a rose
3. a Beethoven symphony
4. a computer
5. the drawings of a young child

26. Love, in Greek and Roman classical works, is equated with

1. piety.
2. altruism.
3. charity.
4. lust.
5. the good.

27. The Greeks and Romans made an analogy between erotic love and

    1.   beauty.
    2.   paradise.
    3.   musical harmony.
    4.   sickness.
    5.   the journey of life.

28. As the concept of God changed in the Hebrew Bible

    1.   God became the role model for the father of the family.
    2.   interest shifted from the good of the group to the good of the individual.
    3.   rules about sexual conduct became liberalized.
    4.   love of the father became less important than fear in preserving the family unit.
    5.   the mother lost authority in the family unit.

29. In the Middle Ages the cult of Mariolatry was responsible for

    1.   a heretical sect denounced by the church.
    2.   the origin of the ideal of romantic love.
    3.   a growing cynicism about idealized love.
    4.   13th century Satan worship.
    5.   realistic depiction of the Virgin.

30. The kind of relationship between men and women portrayed in medieval romances is likened to those in

    1.   the films of the thirties and forties.
    2.   mystical poems about the love of God.
    3.   X-rated films of the eighties.
    4.   commercial films with happy endings.
    5.   the cynical fiction of the naturalists.

31. Castiglione wrote <u>The Courtier</u> as

    1.   cynical advice on the art of seduction.
    2.   satire of the rules of courtly love.
    3.   a guide to the proper conduct of romantic affairs.
    4.   a romantic tale of gallantry.
    5.   an exhortation to be faithful to the marriage vow.

32. In the Restoration period in England

    1.   women were allowed great social freedom.
    2.   adultery was punished by social ostracism.
    3.   the theater supported a rigid sexual morality.
    4.   literature depicted the happy marriage as one in which the husband ruled the household.
    5.   women were expected to be helpless and quite ignorant of the real world.

33. The chapter on love makes the observation that films and books of the 1980s

1. reflect a widespread concern for egotistical satisfaction at any cost to others.
2. suggest an increasingly popular return to traditional family values.
3. reveal society's permissiveness in language and social behavior.
4. show that women are losing the power they gained in the liberation movement.
5. show more tolerance of divorce than did the books and films of the 1970s.

MODULE XI

Themes in the Humanities: Happiness

OVERVIEW

There are as many definitions of happiness as there are of love and other human
ideals. Philosophers have pondered the complexities of this much desired state and
have reached no consensus concerning what it is or how its presence or absence can be
recognized. Some, for example, have made pleasure the core of a happy existence,
while others maintain that happiness is not at all the same as pleasure, that
happiness and pleasure may even be incompatible! Small wonder that so many people
find themselves frustrated. They sometimes feel themselves to be unhappy, even if
they are not sure what it means to be the opposite. Or they give perhaps too narrow
a range to their expectations of happiness. They may equate happiness with perfect
health. They imagine they would be miserable if they were physically handicapped,
but obviously there are many who are deaf or blind or unable to walk and who not only
survive but cannot understand why others pity them. Perhaps the narrowest
measurement of happiness involves counting the number of our material possessions,
but this usually leads us to a state of perpetual dissatisfaction with ourselves and
envy of others who seem to have so much more and also, therefore, must be "happier."
But then there is Aristotle's definition which may come as a surprise and maybe even
a shaft of sunlight to those who struggle to come to some equitable terms with their
existence. Aristotle teaches us that one definition of a happy life has nothing to
do with either the pleasure or pain of daily living but is rather to be found in the
quality of one's total life and in whether it has been lived in wisdom and honor.
This module imparts no final answer to the puzzling questions it asks, but it does
present options we need to consider.

LEARNING OBJECTIVES

Having completed this module, you should be able to

1)   recognize the key elements in hedonism, Epicureanism, Stoicism,
     utilitarianism, and Artistotle's theory of happiness.

2)   define and apply the "big earnings theory" to hedonist values and ways of
     approaching life.

3)   contrast the protagonist's hedonistic approach to happiness in the first
     part of Goethe's Faust to the understanding he reaches at the conclusion of
     the drama.

4)   compare the views of happiness in Camus's Myth of Sisyphus and the
     conclusion of Goethe's Faust.

5) identify an approach to the subject of happiness which is most congenial to your own needs and temperament.

AS YOU READ

Chapter 12: "Happiness"

1. What is hedonism? Summarize four basic assumptions of hedonism. Would you characterize modern day America as hedonistic? Defend your answer.

2. Distinguish between the importance Aristippus and Epicurus attach to pleasure in relation to happiness.

3. What are the ingredients in the Epicurean formula for happiness?

4. What basic assumption of the Stoics regarding human nature underlies and justifies their recommended way of living?

5. It is recorded that Zeno committed suicide after teaching for fifty-eight years. Does suicide seem to be an option more appropriate to a Stoic than to a hedonist?

6. Shortly after the advent of Christianity the philosophy of Stoicism had its greatest impact on Roman thought. What was the underlying premise?

7. What essentials of Stoicism made it congenial to both the Roman and Judeo-Christian minds?

8. What basic assumption about human nature underlies Aristotle's theory of happiness?

9. Upon what chain of reasoning is Aristotle's distinction between pleasure and happiness founded?

10. Some contend that a condition for happiness is the belief in an intelligible order and purpose in the universe. Would your belief that life had no meaning detract from your happiness?

11. Aristotle left out work as a major contributor to happiness. What does the text have to say about contemporary attitudes toward work?

VIEWING

I. In Search of Happiness

--The prologue to Goethe's Faust takes place in heaven before the throne of God. As the angels praise the goodness of creation, Mephistopheles, who is an agent of Satan, criticizes the human race. God agrees that human creatures have weaknesses, but He insists that a good man will be saved by striving in spite of his errors. God selects Faust as a model of the good man. Mephistopheles makes a wager that he can lead Faust to his damnation, using as his weapon human restlessness and perpetual dissatisfaction with life as it is. The viewpoint of Mephistopheles--that humankind is incapable of happiness--is used as a framework for the program.

--The Psalm which is read belongs, apparently, to a very early stage of biblical development, an era in which the Hebraic tribes eked out a hard living from a stingy earth. The view of happiness is rooted in ordinary survival needs, and the additional security of knowing that God is directly conscious of those needs. The often observed mysteriousness of God's actions is, therefore, a parallel theme in the Hebrew Bible reaching its most profound expression in The Book of Job, and it has been a continual source of anguish for religious people.

--Aristotle in his celebrated theory of happiness raises the question: what is man's highest good? The highest good is that which is an end in itself and not desired for the attainment of something else. Only happiness can be defined in this way, for it is self-evident (to Aristotle) that all other things are desired for the sake of happiness, but happiness is never sought for their sake.

--One of the most important aspects of Aristotle's theory is the distinction he makes between happiness and pleasure. Pleasure is certainly a good, for every-one wishes to avoid its opposite, pain. However, pleasure is not self-sufficient; it can be increased by the addition of some other good, like wisdom. Therefore pleasure is not the same as happiness, but one of its ingredients. Happiness consists in the exercise of reason and virtue, since these are the properties that characterize human beings and distinguish them from the animals. For Aristotle, happiness (hence the exercise of virtue and reason) is the reason for living.

--The basic view of the original hedonists was that happiness is pleasure, and pleasure is strictly physical, something of and for the senses. Neither the recollection nor the anticipation of pleasure counts, but only what is actually there to be seen or touched. Later versions of hedonism often concede that other kinds of pleasure are admissible, but the fundamental assumption is still the total selfishness of everything we do. The question to ask oneself is whether one can be happy if someone else's needs are taken care of, not one's own.

--Bentham's hedonic calculus may seem a bit naive, but it does represent an early attempt to "computerize" the elusive subject of happiness. Bentham designed his system to be the basis of actual legislation. If Bentham's plan had been implemented, pleasure would have been controlled and limited. Nonetheless, even though his Utilitarian Party no longer exists, its theory of happiness as the greatest good for the greatest number is still involved in many legislative matters, such as sexual morality, the use of marijuana, etc.

--"Future Shock" is an expression made famous by Alvin Toffler, who used it as the title of a book published in 1970. It refers to the prevalent feeling of confusion and displacement caused by a rate of social change too dizzying for people to adjust to, or as the author defines it, it is "the human response to

overstimulation." Video games, constant noise from transistor radios, blaring
TV sets may suggest a nation of people out for a good time; but if Toffler is
right, they are too far out of touch with their feelings to know whether they
are happy.

--Wordsworth's sonnet "The World Is Too Much With Us" is an anguished expression
of one who cannot enjoy a total commitment to anything. Read it carefully and
ask yourself what the basic problem is and what the poet would like to do about
it.

> The world is too much with us; late and soon,
> Getting and spending, we lay waste our powers:
> Little we see in nature that is ours;
> We have given our hearts away, a sordid boon!
> This Sea that bares her bosom to the moon;
> The winds that will be howling at all hours,
> And are up-gathered now like sleeping flowers;
> For this, for everything, we are out of tune;
> It moves us not. - Great God! I'd rather be
> A Pagan suckled in a creed outworn;
> So might I, standing on this pleasant lea,
> Have glimpses that would make me less forlorn;
> Have sight of Proteus rising from the sea;
> Or hear Old Triton blow his wreathed horn.

--Whitman's poem "When I heard the Learn'd Astronomer" is less complicated, hence
will not be reproduced here. It remains one of the most effective contrasts
between intellectualism and direct experience ("I...looked up in a perfect
silence at the stars" rather than listen to the scientist explain his charts and
diagrams.) This poem, as well as Wordsworth's, is used to illustrate the view
that there is no happiness for one who develops his mind to the exclusion of the
senses and the feelings.

--Marx believed that happiness consists in useful work and having a product to
show for it. The robot-like factory workers shown here will surely not have a
product, but few people do anymore. Do you think relatively meaningless work
leads to boredom and frustration, hence unhappiness? Or should work make the
difference?

--Bertrand Russell says a lazy person can never be happy. Often, people who
retire complain that they are becoming lazy and wish they had something useful
to do. Do you think Russell is right? Do retired people need to "keep busy"
doing useful things in order to be happy? Is this a limited view of what
happiness is all about?

--Thomas Merton, who turned from an active to a contemplative life when he entered
a Trappist monastery, espousing a life of silence, meditation, and physical
labor, is quoted in the program as saying, "You never find happiness until you
stop looking for it." How does one experience happiness by laboring in silence,
without pay or recognition?

--Albert Camus in his "Myth of Sisyphus" describes the endless punishment imposed
upon Sisyphus by the gods--rolling a rock uphill only to have it slide down
again--not as an exercise in futility, but as an example of how attitudes can
create a happy life. One doesn't think about an ultimate product of the labor;

158

one takes each step as it comes and rejoices in the power he has to move the rock. Are there parallels in real life to this uphill rock-rolling?

--We go back to Faust at the program's conclusion. The hero discovers that the true secret of happiness lies not in total intellectual comprehension or in total sensual fulfillment, both of which he has sought, but in responding (like Sisyphus) to the challenge of each moment. Nor are tangible achievement, fame, money, and power the keys to happiness if there is no true involvement in the daily flow of existence.

II. The Intricate Eye

--All of us walk in our own world--the world of our five senses. And we are as free in that world, and as limited as our senses allow. We take for granted that the sense of sight is the dominant one--a prerequisite for happiness. This presentation, however, centers on a person who does not have that sense, who has been sightless from birth and yet manages to live a fulfilling life. She is Leah Howard, an English instructor who also teaches braille. Braille, for Leah, and for many thousands of sightless persons who have learned to read it, is an alternate medium of communication.

--Vision has become for many the undisputed ruler of the senses. The blind, however, walk quietly among us, having to adapt to conditions that assume one can see. Those who aspire to happiness instead of self-pity must accommodate themselves to the fact that their other senses must do their "seeing."

--The various sculptures Leah explores with her fingertips illustrate the amount of information and pleasure transmitted through the tactile sense. People with sight tend to overlook the tactile experiences open to them. While all sculptors do not necessarily want their works handled, there is a way sighted people can add to their own esthetic pleasure through the tactile senses.

--It is not a straightforward matter of sighted people as opposed to nonsighted ones. Once the "intricacy of perception" is recognized, then we realize that all the media of perception have "as much right" to lay claim to THE TRUTH as the medium of sight. This is perhaps the deeper meaning of the title. All of the senses are intricate eyes--windows opening upon endless worlds.

SELF-TEST

Match each item in the first column with an item in the second. Use no item more than one time.

1.   hedonism

2.   Epicurus

3.   Epictetus

4.   Aristotle

5.   color to the blind

6.   ~~Faust~~

7.   Jeremy Bentham

8.   big earnings theory

9.   The Republic

10.   Pitirim Sorokin

11.   objection to Aristotle's theory of happiness

12.   Marx

13,   social consciousness

selfish pleasure-seeking has doomed Western civilization _____

an element lacking in classical theories of happiness _____

happiness is the sum of physical pleasures _____

wisdom and virtue are evidence of the happy life _____

enduring model of utopian ideas _____

adversity can be endured through rational control of emotions _____

happiness is having meaningful work and a product to show for it _12_

happiness is the absence of pain _____

happiness lies in daily striving, not in stupendous achievement _____

happiness is statistically measurable _____

accumulation of richly deserved rewards from life _6_

personal achievement of the good life is not all that matters _____

conception, not perception _____

CHECK LIST OF MAIN IDEAS

1. From the time of the early Greeks, Western philosophers have formulated theories of how best to achieve happiness and/or to cope with pain:

   Aristotle: happiness is man's ultimate goal, arrived at through the continual exercise of virtue and reason.

   Aristippus (hedonism): happiness results solely from physical pleasure--the chief good in life.

   Epicurus (Epicureanism): happiness is achieved more by avoiding pain than by pursuing physical pleasure.

   Zeno, Epictetus (Stoicism): one may minimize pain by remaining indifferent to it.

   Bentham (utilitarianism): the aim of life is to achieve the largest possible excess of pleasure over pain without harming others--in short, the greatest good for the greatest number.

   Marx (dialectical materialism): happiness is achieved through useful work and having a product to show for it.

2. The case of Leah Howard, the blind teacher, suggests that happiness does not always depend on the perfect functioning of the body. If one is, for example, blind from birth, one defines happiness in terms of the goals that are within reach.

3. We have a choice to make: we can risk the consequences of freely pursuing our individual goals or we can submit ourselves to the dictates of a society managed to provide the greatest possible degree of happiness.

4. In general, the humanist would opt for cautious commitment to ideals and freedom of individual action to the degree that it does not infringe upon the free choice of others.

RECOMMENDED READING

Aristotle. <u>Nichomachean Ethics</u> (Appears in various editions and translations). Probably Aristotle's most readable work, containing not only his theory of happiness but observations on almost every moral question that still haunts us.

Sophie Freud. <u>My Three Mothers and Other Passions</u> (New York: New York University Press, 1988). The granddaughter of the famed psychoanalyst presents her views, some quite unexpected, on the nature of the fulfilled life.

Johann Wolfgang von Goethe. <u>Faust</u>. (Appears in various editions and translations). Most readers are familiar with Part I involving the hero's pact with Mephistopheles, but it is Part II which is relevant to this module.

Thomas Merton. <u>The Seven Storey Mountain</u> (New York: Harcourt, Brace, 1948). The spiritual autobiography of a man who gave up many worldly advantages to become a Trappist monk.

Alvin Toffler. <u>Future Shock</u> (New York: Random House, 1970). A detailed analysis of our present sense of alienation in terms of the accelerating rate of change.

MODULE XII

Themes in the Humanities: Coping with Death

OVERVIEW

Until recently death has not been a popular subject. It was a dread event to be mentioned only in its poetic and literary senses, or confronted in the movies. There is a new attitude emerging, however: if life is to be lived as fully and as richly as possible, people must confront their death attitudes, their fears about not only personal extinction and the loss of others, but also about aging and major life transitions. Only in this way can they begin to locate sources of life affirmation. There have always been beliefs in immortality, found in mythology and religion. But there are growing indications of scientific support for transcending the fear of death. Recent investigations indicate that death may actually be not fearful at all but perhaps even the beautiful experience cynics once said was possible only in poetic fantasy.

LEARNING OBJECTIVES

Having completed this module, you should be able to

1) identify reasons for the fear of death in Western society.

2) contrast attitudes toward dying and/or the rituals of death in rural and metropolitan areas, and in Eastern and Western societies.

3) define the various "death attitudes" as psychologically debilitating forces.

4) identify life-denying elements in our society which spring from death attitudes.

5) explain recent investigations into the nature of dying.

6) identify resources for life affirmation in nature, religion, mythology, and the arts.

7) explain the relationship between the cyclical form and the resurrection theme.

8) recognize theories that have been used in literature and philosophy to account for the presence of death and other phenomena considered to be evils.

163

Chapter 13: "Coping With Death"

1. How are attitudes toward death different from death attitudes?

2. Formulate an acceptable rule of thumb which relates the concept of self to an attitude toward death.

3. The point is made, using Socrates as a prime example, that where activities become more important than personalities, the fear of death can be surmounted. How is this possible?

4. Contrast Medieval and Renaissance attitudes toward death.

5. The ideal of glorious death sustained humanity for centuries. Is it still around? Why, or why not?

6. What are some prevalent religious views on suicide? What point does Dr. Parsons make about self-inflicted death?

7. Does religion tend to support a fatalistic attitude toward death?

8. How do you think hedonistic elements in contemporary U. S. society color our attitudes towards life and death? How are they manifested?

9. The chapter analyzes several forms of symbolic death. Give examples of behavior that characterizes symbolic suicide; symbolic murder; burn-out.

10. What theory is presented in the text to account for the fear of aging, which is so pronounced in America?

11. Give one or two examples of "Phoenix models"--that is, ways to achieve a sense of life affirmation.

VIEWING

I. <u>For Everything, a Season</u>

--In Western society, despite the affirmative character of Judeo-Christian theology, death is generally regarded as the ultimate tragedy. To a considerable extent, this results from our one-sided emphasis on the material satisfactions of life, from the values we attach to money, possessions, getting ahead, status, and power. These, in the popular conception, represent the fulfillment of life. To lose any of them becomes a kind of death in life. And finally to lose all of them to death itself signifies ultimate failure.

--Youth, too, ranks high in our scale of satisfactions; the world, we tell ourselves, belongs to the young. Life is sweetest when one's strength, good

looks, passions, and expectations are at their highest. But once the crest of
youth is passed, we are ready to see existence as all downhill from then on.
The frantic attempt to hold fast to (the illusion of) youth and retard
(supposedly) the aging process is one of our major forms of life-denial.

--The Pompeiian Principle is another of our major death attitudes. Borrowing its
label from the pleasure oriented city at the foot of Mt. Vesuvius, the principle
tells us that time is running out, nothing ultimately matters, and one should
live for the moment alone. While the viewer may decide for himself just how
useful it is in his own life, one should note that the Pompeiian Principle has
been around a long while. Ours is not the first society to decide that there
isn't much time left.

--The fear of hell's fire was surely great at the time Shakespeare created
Hamlet's famous soliloquy and even greater during the Puritan era in our own
history. No doubt this has often contributed to an ambiguous relationship with
the next world. One wonders whether current concerns emphasize instead the
possibility of everlasting joy or whether the afterlife remains a viable concept
at all, even for many of the faithful caught up as they are in the "nowness" of
contemporary thinking.

--The New Orleans jazz funeral shown here is absolutely authentic. The footage
comes from the newsroom of a New Orleans station. The passing of Louis
Armstrong was marked by just such a pageant. Do you find the apparent levity
(the dancing in the streets, drinking beer, etc.) disrespectful toward the dead?
Should such rituals be more solemn and majestic?

--Eastern philosophers see death as neither evil nor good. It is an event--a
different version of birth. Definitions of death, Eastern thought maintains,
are but human inventions, and the mind becomes trapped in their limitations.
Yet we are assured that it is within our power to see death in any light we
choose.

--There are some indications that the living-room wake is becoming a thing of the
past in some rural areas, but the generalization may still be made that the
presence of death seems less tolerable in large cities with mobile populations
than in country places where large families remain tied to the land for
generations. It also appears to be true that in such places children confront
the fact of death at a very early age--a "passage" greatly admired by most
psychologists.

--In urbanized Western culture there are three major reasons for the fear of
death:

1)   the loss of personal identity. Western culture has always stressed
     individualism. Its history is often said to be the record of what
     great persons have done. To labor all of one's life to achieve
     importance and then to be gone from the scene strikes the Western mind
     as a crowning insult--a cosmic injustice.
2)   the thought that many of us entertain--of lying alone in a grave,
     being far away from people we love. We place a high value on love and
     togetherness. Death is antisocial, antifamily.
3)   the fear of passing through death's door, the actual experience of
     dying. What will it be like? Will I suffer?

165

II.   <u>The Problem of Evil</u>

--"Evil" in the title is used in the broadest sense of the term, referring to
human suffering as well as to moral corruption. The random occurrence of
suffering, the apparently indiscriminate manner in which the innocent seem to
suffer in this life, has traditionally troubled the moral and religious
philosophers.

--There is a dramatization of scenes from Herman Melville's novel, <u>Moby Dick</u>.
Starting with an adventure yarn about a whaling voyage, Melville expanded the
story until it became a titanic myth about humanity's tragic failure to comprehend a universe of terrifying force that may be operated by no God at all or
by a malevolent one.

--Reference is made to Thomas Aquinas's proofs of the existence of God. Aquinas
believed that, while faith was necessary for the devout, reason was also a gift
of God by means of which the human intellect could achieve positive confirmation
of what faith already knew. Thomism--still very much with us--is often utilized
by priests to convince agnostics that the rational mind has no alternative but
to accept the truths taught by the Church.

--The poem read by the narrator is by the Spanish mystic, St. John of the Cross.
The title may be translated, "Verses upon Ecstasy of High Contemplation." The
fame of the poet rests upon his ability to describe in metaphor and imagery an
experience that cannot otherwise be explained.

--Pascal, a 17th century philosopher, believed that God could be known through a
mystic certainty and that a psychological need filled by religious mysticism was
more important than rational certainty.

--Baruch (also known as Benedict) Spinoza (1632-1677) was born in Amsterdam into a
family of refugee Jews from Spain and Portugal. Raised in a tradition of
orthodox Judaism, Spinoza later incurred the wrath and suffered excommunication
at the hands of the faithful by postulating that, since God was omnipotent,
everything in the universe must be an attribute of God. In other words, Spinoza
denied a separation between Creator and creation. In so doing. he denied the
absolute existence of evil.

--Voltaire's satirical novel <u>Candide</u> (1759) was written, among other reasons, to
counteract what its author considered to be the absurd optimism of some 18th
century philosophers, especially Gottfried Wilhelm von Leibnitz, who coined the
famous (and infamous) description of the earth as the best of all possible
worlds. The earthquake at Lisbon occurred on November 1, 1755. Some 30,000-
50,000 people were killed, many while they attended church. The Philosophy of
Optimism (e.g. Leibnitz) viewed such disasters as working for an eventual,
compensating good. Voltaire was outraged by the complacency with which such a
philosophy accepted the suffering of human beings and denied the value of human
effort in the world.

--The woman in the bird-like white mask is Cunegonde, Candide's long-lost love, in
disguise, she who takes Candide into her home and cares for him after his
"ritual" flogging.

166

--As you can see from Voltaire's handling of Church authorities and the Inquisition, the author of <u>Candide</u> was not very much in sympathy with any attempts, religious or otherwise, to gain control of people's minds. The extent to which he thought the Church in particular could distort and manipulate reality to suit its own needs is shown by the absurd charges brought against the unfortunate prisoners selected at random in order for the Church to gain "official" vengeance for the earthquake.

--When Bill asks the question, "What kind of God would allow such waste?" he considers several theories offered as reasons for innocent suffering: God has mysterious reasons for permitting evil to exist; God is powerless to prevent evil; God is omnipotent but is indifferent to human suffering; what happens to us is the result of blind chance, and there is no purpose to our suffering.

--Toward the end of the program, the priest talks about a possible effect of the devastating suffering of human beings in the Nazi death camps--that is, that such suffering gives people a chance to show compassion, a very human dimension that might not be called for under ordinary circumstances.

--When Bill asks the priest for an answer to the question of innocent suffering, note that the point of the conversation is not that the priest is unable to answer the question, but that Bill has perhaps failed to ask the right questions.

Match each item in the first column with an item in the second. Use no item more than one time.

T	1.	Socratic attitude toward death	critical of how society treats the dying	_____
T	2.	John Calvin	gossip	_____
T	3.	famous for patience	often concludes on note of merrymaking	_____
V	4.	professional science for coping with death	thanatology	_____
V	5.	Elisabeth Kübler-Ross	time is running out	_____
T	6.	motivated by excessive sense of personal unworth	a symbolic tale about the enigma of evil	_____
T	7.	mythological creature often used as symbol of rebirth	pursuit of wisdom greater than loss of individual	_____
V	8.	New Orleans funeral	finds death neither good nor evil	_____
V	9.	Pompeiian principle	Job	_____
V	10.	Eastern philosophy	symbolic suicide	_____
V	11.	Voltaire	poet of life affirmation	_____
T	12.	Edward Arlington Robinson	Phoenix	_____
V	13.	Moby Dick	human life predetermined from cradle to grave	_____
T	14.	symbolic murder	satirized philosophy of optimism	_____

CHECK LIST OF MAIN IDEAS

1. Historically humanity has dealt with death in varying ways: by glorifying it (mortal man approaches the gods when he dies a heroic death); by denying it (life continues after death in either heaven or hell); by viewing it as simply another phenomenon, neither good nor evil.

2. To many people, if no meaning can be found for innocent suffering, the universe itself appears random and pointless.

3. How we live life affects how we view death: self-centered hedonists have difficulty coping with death; self-denying Buddhists and persons to whom activities are more important than personalities accept death with equanimity.

4. Death attitudes engendered by feelings of unworth affect our own and others' lives. By following self-destructive paths (e.g., compulsive drinking), we commit symbolic suicide; by reveling in the misfortune of others (e.g., vicious gossip) we commit symbolic murder. A sense of failure often manifests itself in a desperate fear of aging.

5. Humanists seek life-affirming strategies (Phoenix models) whereby they may revive the spirit and reaffirm their dedication to living--among such strategies, a periodic decision to forgive themselves for past misdirections.

RECOMMENDED READING

The Book of Job. Considered by many to be the major work of the Hebrew Bible--a
   tough-minded statement on the meaning of divine providence and the eternal
   limitations in the human understanding of God.

Stephen Crane. The Red Badge of Courage (New York: Holt, Rinehart and Winston,
   1968). A short but powerful novel about a young man's romantic view of dying
   heroically in war--and how he discovers the grim reality.

Robert Fulton, et al. ed. Death and Dying Challenge and Change (Reading, Mass.:
   Addison-Wesley Publishing Co., 1978).

Elisabeth Küber-Ross. On Death and Dying (New York: Macmillan, 1969). In this her
   most influential work, the Swiss-born thanatologist analyzes the American
   neurosis on the subject of death, especially the shameful treatment our society
   gives to the elderly and the dying.

_____. Death: The Final Stage of Growth (Englewood Cliffs, N.J.,
   Prentice-Hall, 1975).

Jessica Mitford. The American Way of Death (New York: Simon and Shuster, 1963). An
   Englishwoman's not too complimentary observations on funerals as a major
   profit-making industry in the United States.

William Shakespeare. Hamlet (Appears in various editions). Shakespeare's most
   death-oriented tragedy--in terms of the amount of time devoted to speculations
   on the mysterious journey that awaits everyone.

Leo Tolstoy. The Death of Ivan Ilych (New York: New American Library, 1960). A
   graphic and exhausting study of terminal illness, leaving the reader in a
   strangely peaceful mood of complete catharsis.

Thornton Wilder. Our Town (New York: Harper and Row, 1957). One of the greatest of
   all American plays--a simple yet profound statement about the cycle of birth and
   death and the everlasting fitness of things.

1. It is most characteristic of the Epicurean, in his search for happiness to

    1. put the highest value on intensity of pleasure rather than duration.
    2. measure the amount of happiness by a kind of hedonistic calculus.
    3. measure happiness by the absence of pain.
    4. measure happiness by whether the greatest amount for the greatest number is created.
    5. make a distinction between pleasure and happiness.

2. Which of the following statements is based most directly on Aristotle's view of happiness?

    1. Pleasure can in no way bring us happiness.
    2. If you want happiness, don't try to find it with money.
    3. In moderate amounts, pleasure and money are absolutely essential to happiness.
    4. Since we desire pleasure for the sake of happiness, it follows that happiness and pleasure cannot be the same thing.
    5. The definition of happiness depends upon individual taste and experience.

3. Epicurus was greatly interested in the hedonistic approach to life. At length he rejected its underlying premises. One of his major reasons for so doing was that

    1. it would be impossible to live long enough to enjoy a sufficient number of pleasures.
    2. the hedonist failed to distinguish between what was and was not permissible by law.
    3. some hedonistic pleasures were no doubt counter to religious commandments.
    4. conformity to society's demands is more conducive to peace of mind in the long run.
    5. to his knowledge no devout hedonist of the past had ever been recognized for distinguished achievements.

4. The 19th century Utilitarians comprised an actual political party based on a philosophy and dedicated to the promise of bringing about legislation to promote something they felt the state should guarantee. What was it?

1. a higher education for every citizen
2. freedom from invasion of privacy
3. an end of militarism
4. the greatest good for the greatest number
5. a minimum annual wage to paid by the government out of a tax on colonial holdings

5. We can often identify elements of our personal philosophy by the way we respond to newspaper headlines. Which of the following headlines would probably make you the MOST happy and LEAST depressed?

   1. GASOLINE BAN ON LEISURE DRIVING LIFTED
   2. MARKET STABLE AFTER WEEK WITHOUT DISTURBING NEWS
   3. THREAT OF NEW MIDEAST VIOLENCE EASES
   4. NEW SERVICE CORPS APPROVED. APPLICANTS MUST SERVE MINIMUM OF FIVE YEARS
   5. CHARITY TELETHON SCANDAL EXPOSED, SEVEN TO FACE CHARGES

6. The sequence in which the little girl buries the dead bird in For Everything, a Season indicates that a possible reaction to death is

   1. viewing it as part of the natural cycle.
   2. attempting to conceal the fact of death.
   3. bargaining with life.
   4. searching for religious transcendence.
   5. creating a Phoenix myth.

7. While it is dangerous to make sweeping generalizations, people in the East tend to look upon death far differently from people in the West. Which of the following statements of contrast is probably most accurate?

   1. The image of death as soft reeds in a gentle river is more likely to appear in Western literature.
   2. An Eastern funeral would be marked by long eulogies to the departed.
   3. A Western funeral would be marked by considerable reserve and very little show of grief.
   4. A Buddhist would probably regard someone's death as simply another phenomenon with which to deal.
   5. Children in middle-class New York homes have probably had their first encounter with death by the time they are five.

8. The purposes of playing jazz and dancing in the streets in a New Orleans jazz funeral is most likely that

   1. one ought to concentrate on the living, not the dead.
   2. life is a farce, so why not live it up?
   3. we must rejoice that the departed is free from life's pain.
   4. we should send off the departed by playing music that was most familiar to him.
   5. playing happy music will help us to keep our true feelings under control.

9. All of the following probably represent life-denying actions except

   1. spreading gossip about your neighbors.

2. refusing to buy an admired outfit because it is inappropriate for your age.
3. trying to double your paycheck at the race track every Friday.
4. attending a bullfight.
5. driving at excessive speeds.

10. The greatest likelihood that the sudden, unexpected death of a close friend can be overcome occurs when

1. the survivor has a wide circle of friends.
2. the survivor had not needed the departed to reinforce his own identity.
3. the departed had shown courage in the face of death.
4. the departed had lived a respectable number of years.
5. the survivor had actually been present at the moment of death.

11. Recent scientific investigations into the nature of dying reveal that the ancient Tibetan Book of the Dead had some rather remarkable insights, especially concerning which of the following?

1. out-of-body experiences
2. the geography of the next world
3. the reunion with loved ones at the instant of passing
4. a sudden sense of hostility toward earthly life
5. an anxiety about reward and punishment

12. Hamlet's "to be or not to be" soliloquy expresses an attitude concerning death which has not been uncommon in Western society for many centuries. It is that

1. if death is going to happen, it is going to happen.
2. one must fear death because the next world, if there is one, is an unknown quantity.
3. it is certainly better to die than to suffer "the slings and arrows of outrageous fortune."
4. death cuts everyone down to the same size.
5. a sleep of oblivion would be far worse than hell's fire.

13. Those who have made studies of death attitudes in Western culture have concluded that considerable differences exist in the way rural and urban people react to death. Which of the following statements of contrast is probably most accurate?

1. Urban people are more likely to feel that life should continue as before and less likely to cling to past memories.
2. Rural people are more likely to fear death because it is an interruption of a stable way of life.
3. Because of the greater mobility of urban populations, people in the city are more likely to spend time with the dying.
4. Rural people are more likely, and at an earlier age, to be accustomed to the presence of death.
5. No significant difference exists.

14. In the TV program For Everything, a Season, the point was made that in urbanized Western culture death is generally feared for all of the following reasons EXCEPT

173

1. death means the loss of personal identity.
2. dying may be painful.
3. death means being away from the people we love.
4. death is a release from suffering.
5. death represents ultimate failure.

15. The symbol of the Phoenix appears over and over in literature and mythology, but there are many actions people perform which can also suggest a symbolic form of resurrection. Which of the following could be called a Phoenix symbol?

    1. the rank ordering of college football teams
    2. selling real estate for a significant profit
    3. completing a college degree at the age of 70
    4. replacing a low-rent housing project with a multi-storied shopping center
    5. replacing a cancer research center with a physical fitness center

16. Ours is a period dominated by the Pompeiian Principle - an approach to living delineated in the program For Everything, a Season. Which of the following BEST defines that principle?

    1. feeling desperately that time is running out
    2. living in the past
    3. intensifying the enjoyment of life through collecting lasting works of art
    4. engaging in periodic forgiveness rituals
    5. burying the dead amid joyful music and street dancing

17. All of the following are applicable to Stoicism EXCEPT that

    1. happiness is a matter of how we respond to what happens.
    2. to find the roots of happiness one should look inward.
    3. humans are free to change events in the world process.
    4. nothing is under our control, except the way we feel about things.
    5. if anyone is unhappy, it's his own fault.

18. The "Hedonic Calculus" was devised

    1. to measure the pleasurable consequences of acts.
    2. to make philosophy an exact science.
    3. to reach absolute truth through mathematics.
    4. to offer a rational attack on hedonism.
    5. to prove mathematically that happiness was an illogical human ideal.

19. At the conclusion of The Problem of Evil Bill suggests to the priest that perhaps he has not yet started to ask the right questions concerning the nature and reason for evil in the world. Which of the following options (all of which may have equal validity) strikes you as being the most meaningful "right" question Bill could ask?

    1. Is the random suffering of innocent people the same thing as "evil"?
    2. May not "unfair," applied to the suffering of the innocent, be an idea in my own mind?
    3. May it not be that I have offended God in ways of which I am unaware?
    4. Is it not possible that death, at whatever age it comes, is not to be regarded as an evil?

174

5. Is it not possible that I will meet someone else whom I will love better and that the thought of doing so is in no way sacrilegious to the memory of my wife?

20. In the program In Search of Happiness an episode was taken from a work by Goethe. Its final message was that "he only deserves freedom and happiness who wins them over in the labor of every day." Which character found this to be true?

    1. Mephistopheles
    2. Oedipus
    3. Hamlet
    4. Faust
    5. Chaplin

21. The meaning of the observation quoted in the preceding question is that

    1. happiness comes from responding to continual challenges, not from ultimate results.
    2. happiness is made up of the little ordinary things that happen to us daily.
    3. there can be no happiness unless one has reached a major goal and fulfilled a great dream
    4. people who work for a living are happier than those who live on inherited wealth.
    5. you will be happy as long as you are free.

22. Several passages from Hamlet in Chapter 13 illustrate an attitude found frequently in Shakespeare's work. It is that

    1. since death makes us all equal, the achievements of a lifetime are ultimately futile.
    2. since death is a natural part of life, there is no need to fear it.
    3. we must each personally decide whether the journey of life has any final meaning.
    4. no harm can come to a good man in life or in death.
    5. since death is inevitable, we should make creative and productive use of life while we have it.

23. An idea that John Calvin bestowed on American Puritanism is that

    1. we are free to choose between good and evil.
    2. we are predestined to salvation or damnation.
    3. chance rules everything.
    4. we cannot know if there is an afterlife, but we must act as if there is.
    5. no good deed goes unpunished.

24. A form of symbolic death is linked in the text especially with professionals who once were creative and energetic but are so no longer: What is it?

    1. risk taking
    2. fear of aging
    3. claiming to be "born again"
    4. fatalism
    5. burn out

175

25. Voltaire's satiric novel <u>Candide</u> pokes fun at a viewpoint that was very popular during the eighteenth century and that is voiced by the hero's teacher, Dr. Pangloss. It is that

    1. God would return before the end of the century.
    2. this is a universe of sheer random chance, without meaning.
    3. happiness comes from facing life without desires.
    4. human nature is basically depraved and is incapable of improvement.
    5. everything happens for the best.

26. The assumption that people never get as much pleasure as they deserve is characteristic of the thinking of

    1. Epicurus.
    2. hedonists.
    3. stoics.
    4. Aristotle.
    5. Plato.

27. Lacking in classical Greek and Roman thinking about happiness is a concern for

    1. the well-being of others.
    2. the role of pleasure in achieving happiness.
    3. the relationship between pleasure and pain.
    4. the inevitability of death.
    5. the transitoriness of pleasure.

28. The theory that links happiness with productive and meaningful work is attributed to

    1. B. F. Skinner.
    2. Thomas Merton.
    3. Karl Marx.
    4. Jeremy Bentham.
    5. Camus.

29. For Aristotle "the good" does not include

    1. virtue.
    2. wisdom.
    3. friendship.
    4. love.
    5. health.

30. The philosophy of Stoicism is associated with

    1. Plato.
    2. Aristotle.
    3. Epictetus.
    4. Bentham.
    5. Aristippus.

31. To Aristotle the state existed

1. to protect the property of citizens against foreigners and slaves.
2. to promote the happiness of the citizen.
3. to care for the disadvantaged.
4. to patronize the arts.
5. to protect the natural environment.

32. Which of the following, in your opinion, best explains the meaning of the title The Intricate Eye?

    1. Any of our senses can function in place of one that is missing.
    2. Non-sighted people "see" a great deal more than sighted people.
    3. No two people see anything precisely the same way.
    4. One's own happiness is enhanced by the ability to feel empathy for those who experience life in a different way.
    5. The meaning of the verb to see should not be confined to the possession of physical sight.

33. Which of the following approximates your own view of happiness?

    1. I will be happy only if I am attractive, healthy, and financially secure.
    2. Happiness is impossible without the presence of someone to love and be loved by in return.
    3. Happiness lies in being content with one's lot in life.
    4. The truly happy are those who serve humanity.
    5. Happiness is never being bored.

34. At one point Leah Howard is asked whether she would like to possess the sense of sight. Her response is negative. Which of the following is PROBABLY the reason?

    1. She gets along well enough without sight.
    2. Her teaching specialty is braille.
    3. There is nothing she would really like to see.
    4. Sight objects, like faces, have no meaning for her.
    5. She would become disoriented.

MODULE XIII

Themes in the Humanities: Apollo and Dionysus

OVERVIEW

One of the graces of the philosopher is the ability to point out to the rest of us a vital truth by which we may come to understand ourselves and our world better. Often the clues we need are simpler that we ever dreamed. Such is the case with Nietzsche's perception of the significance to human life of the ancient Greek gods, Apollo and Dionysus. Far from being long-dead mythical beings, these extraordinary creations represent two fundamental polarities in humanity's inner being.

Our Apollonian component represents reason, order, and planning--products of the intellect; whereas our Dionysian side tends toward passion, disorder, destruction--but also creativity. Each approach has its merits and faults. The strict Apollonian way yields stability, but tends to stifle intuition and novel ideas. A truly Dionysian attitude, on the other hand, would allow for freedom to develop new ideas but, alas, these very ideas could be lost in the accompanying chaos. The ideal is to balance these two forces, capturing the best of each.

The implications of the Apollonian and Dionysian aspects of our nature are endless: they shape our life-styles; they activate social movements; they influence the arts, sciences, and philosophy. This interaction of opposing elements, this pendulum-like shifting back and forth from one extreme to the other, expresses the rational and non-rational needs of human existence.

LEARNING OBJECTIVES

Having completed this module, you should be able to

1) summarize Nietzche's psychological applications of the myths of Apollo and Dionysus.

2) relate Apollo and Dionysus to familiar aspects of human life, including education and leisure time activities.

3) Point out the disadvantages of remaining at either extreme in the development of a society, a cause, an individual's personality.

4) explain the concepts of the Apollonian and Dionysian as forces in art and the structuring of social institutions.

5) explain a theory of history which accounts for human events in terms of the oscillation between these two poles.

179

6) identify Dionysian and Apollonian elements in Thomas Mann's <u>Death in Venice</u> and William Golding's <u>Lord of the Flies</u>.

7) explain Rousseau's objection to the emphasis on the Apollonian in the structure of tragic dramas such as <u>Oedipus Rex</u>.

8) contrast the importance placed by Aristotle and Nietzsche on the Apollonian element in life and art.

9) state reasons for historians' considering the fifth century b.c. in Athens to be a perfect era.

10) apply your knowledge of Apollonian and Dionysian forces to an explanation of certain historical events or literary works.

11) enumerate those characteristics of the present period which lead some historians to conclude that Western society is presently living through a predominantly Dionysian period.

AS YOU READ

Chapter 14: "Apollo and Dionysus"

1. In Greek mythology Apollo, the sun god, represents all that is rational, orderly, and disciplined in life, while Dionysus, the god of vegetation (particularly wine) represents all that is intuitive, spontaneous, and creative. Though these gods were part of the humanistic education of all people for centuries, it was Nietzsche, the 19th century German philosopher, who reviewed their characteristics and found Apollo and Dionysus useful for naming the two conflicting aspects of human personality.

2. Apollonians tend to be critical, detached, and capable of noticing many subtleties; they revere order. Dionysians tend to be accepting, open to life, and often not very discriminating; they revel in sensuous experience. Why is the extreme of either side to be avoided?

3. Explain the difference between an Apollonian and a Dionysian walk through a forest.

4. How does Zorba the Greek typify the Dionysian spirit?

5. Why is an understanding of Apollo and Dionysis helpful in a humanities course?

6. What examples of contemporary music and drama lead some observers to conclude that we are living in a predominantly Dionysian age?

7. Who tends to "get into" religion more wholeheartedly--the Apollonian or the Dionysian?

8. Identify Apollonian and Dionysian elements in religious beliefs and practices that are cited in the text and some that you can observe in your community.

9. Nietzsche's famous distinction between Apollo and Dionysus occurs in his work, The Birth of Tragedy, and he used the two labels as means of identifying contrasting ways of responding to tragedy. How do Apollonians and Dionysians respond? Which response do you think Nietzsche favors?

10. The text describes a tension that exists in poetry between a Dionysian urge to explode and an Apollonian form that controls the rebellious passion. Can you distinguish these elements in the poems quoted in the text?

11. Was Rousseau Apollonian or Dionysian in his writings?

12. According to the text, do the lower grades in school tend to be mainly Apollonian, mainly Dionysian, or a combination of both?

13. Describe the Dionysian approach in higher education. What Apollonian short-comings is it intended to offset? Are you in agreement with it?

14. What is meant by the statement that "the pure Dionysian teacher does not exist"?

VIEWING

I. Sunlit Chariot: The Apollonian Order in Human Life

   --The opening sequence of this presentation, like that of its companion piece on Dionysus, serves as a dramatic metaphor of the major concepts presented. "Cosmic" events taking place in the mini-universe of the atom, where positive and negative forces hold one another in balance, imply the essential nature of all created phenomena, including man, in whom similar polarities exits.

   --"The Apollonian intellect, striving to understand and to control the power of the atom, discovered a way of interrupting the system that holds the energy in check." Doubtless no more frightening paradox exists today than the fact that science, the most "rational" and Apollonian of our endeavors, has been the means of releasing the most destructive Dionysian force we know: the atom bomb.

   --The American Puritans are used as prime examples of the Apollonian temperament, for not only did they value order and discipline in all phases of life, but they openly persecuted Dionysian lapses within their community. Many Apollonian aspects in the personality of the average American--notably a respect for industriousness and thrift--can be traced to the Puritan legacy.

   --Europe's 18th century, which gave us the term "civilization," coined by one of its most brilliant figures, Dr. Samuel Johnson, is recognized as a period of Apollonian enlightenment. It was an age characterized by intellectual excite-ment, bold scientific discovery, lively inquiry in the fields of philosophy, politics, and the arts. It inspired the founders of American democracy, yet it also demonstrated how swiftly virtue can decline into defect, enlightenment into a cold formalism which leaves no room for alternate vision. The century ended in the violent explosion of the French Revolution, a Dionysian upheaval that left Europe in turmoil for thirty years.

--Another paradox emerges in the conflict between Apollo and Dionysus. When Apollonian values attempt to eject opposing elements from their midst, they can destroy the very values they wish to protect. The Sacco-Vanzetti case, discussed in this connection, reminds us how law, untempered by an understanding of human worth, can become blind and unjust.

Yet, we must also remember, without some measure of Apollonian control, humanity becomes debauched and, in the extreme case, murderous. It is for the protection of life and Dionysian liberty that the Apollonian mind codified social and religious laws.

II.   Dionysus: Ectasy and Renewal

--The opening scene, which shows three boys on a beach, constructing and then destroying a sand castle, is a symbolic representation of the program's theme: the alternation between periods of order and disorder in society and in the individual's personality. Note that the leader of this trio is named Dennis-- surely meant to suggest Dionysus.

--"History...is an account of psychological events." History can be viewed in a variety of ways, and one of them is to view it as cyclical, seeing human events as large rhythmic movements in time resembling the rise and fall of waves. Apollonian rigidity forces Dionysian eruption; Dionysian excesses generate Apollonian control, sometimes more rigid than before.

--It has become traditional to chart the course of Athenian civilization in terms of Apollo and Dionysus. Thus post-Homeric Athens (from the 7th century to the 5th century before Christ) is seen as a period of Apollonian rationality, suitable to the flowering of a culture. The late 5th century, known as the Golden Age of Pericles, is marked by an extraordinary balance between Apollonian rationality and Dionysian zest for living, after which Athenian civilization entered a period increasingly dominated by Dionysian excess. It is this period which is described in the program.

--The modern novel used to illustrate the Dionysian spirit is Thomas Mann's Death in Venice. The sequence depicted in the program is a re-creation of its intellectual hero's dream in which the suppressed Dionysian side of his personality finally asserts itself.

--The Roman feast known as the Saturnalia and, later, the medieval Christian carnival were legalized Dionysian outbursts which made possible the prolongation of Apollonian control. Carnival occurred before the beginning of the Apollonian Lenten season, supposedly marked by fasting and other forms of self-control. In New Orleans, the Mardi Gras ("Fat Tuesday") is a notable survival of ancient tradition. The celebration, which now goes on for about ten days, reaches a frenzied climax the day before Ash Wednesday.

--The arts comprise a vast area in which Apollonian and Dionysian forces can readily be identified. The program singles out some sublime Dionysian achievements: Mark Twain's rebellious Huck Finn, who came along at the height of America's "Gilded" Age, that late 19th century period marked by the emergence of a moneyed aristocracy and distinctly Apollonian standards of taste and conduct; and Beethoven's surging "Ode to Joy," a virtual Dionysian anthem, called by its composer a "pious song in praise of Bacchus."

SELF-TEST

Match each item in the first column with an item in the second. Use no item more than one time.

T	1.	Tennessee Williams	santería	_____
T	2.	Apollonian philosophy	the sun	_____
T	3.	Dionysian religion	second thoughts about a bomb	_____
T	4.	Zorba the Greek	emphasizes morality and organized worship	_____
T	5.	Rousseau	Mardi Gras	_____
T	6.	Dionysian education	Victorians	_____
T	7.	Apollo, god of...	schoolboys revert to primitive beings	_____
V	8.	Einstein	Dionysian/Apollonian paradox	_____
VT	9.	Dionysian festival	art should provoke, not entertain	_____
V	10.	Lord of the Flies	used Apollo and Dionysus as themes	_____
T	11.	Apollonian religion	tends to dominate schools	_____
V	12.	art should morally improve audience	song "in praise of Bacchus"	_____
V	13.	Europe in the 18th century	dances when a business scheme fails	_____
V	14.	"Ode to Joy"	an Apollonian's Dionysian dream	_____
V	15.	Death in Venice	will break the rules in the interest of creativity	_____

183

CHECK LIST OF MAIN IDEAS

1. People's personalities and their subsequent actions stem from an amalgam of two opposing forces: Apollonian, (the embodiment of reason, discipline, or stability) and Dionysian (representing passion, change, or chaos).

2. History reveals that civilization has swung back and forth between these two extremes--with one extreme setting the stage for begetting the other.

3. The ideal human life balances Dionysian passion with Apollonian order.

4. Education represents a crucial battlefield in the intense struggle between Apollo and Dionysus for domination.

5. A strong Dionysian impulse can be observed in contemporary culture.

RECOMMENDED READING

William Golding. Lord of the Flies (New York: Coward, McCann, 1962). The
     Apollonian nature is the superficial trapping of civilization. Humanity is
     fundamentally Dionysian: savage, fiercely competitive, and destructive. At
     least this is the underlying premise of this celebrated novel about a group of
     upper-class English schoolboys who manage to survive a plane crash on a remote
     island.

Nikos Kazantzakis. Zorba the Greek tr. Carl Wildman (New York: Simon & Shuster,
     1952). The definitive novel about an Apollonian/Dionysian relationship. Zorba
     is a modern incarnation of Dionysus himself--passionate, irresistible, and
     irresponsible. His Apollonian friend is a British poet--sober, methodical,
     puritanical, and in Zorba's opinion, incapable of being happy.

Thomas Mann. Death in Venice tr. H. Lowe-Porter (New York: Vintage Books, 1964).
     The hero, a German author with a repressive Apollonian personality, travels to
     Venice, a city of Dionysian sensuality. He unfolds in ways he cannot fully
     comprehend or deal with, and the imbalance inside him leads to tragedy.

Freidrich Nietzsche. The Birth of Tragedy (See Recommended Reading, Module IV).

Robert M. Pirsig. Zen and the Art of Motorcycle Maintenance (New York: Morrow,
     1979). Already a modern classic, this intriguing autobiography of a human
     intellect makes profound comments about the Apollonian life.

Mark Twain. The Adventures of Huckleberry Finn (Appears in various editions).
     Considered by many as "the Great American Novel," Twain's masterpiece gives us a
     hero who sums up the Dionysian side of the American character: its restlessness
     and unwillingness to be fenced in by authority.

Themes in the Humanities: The Mechanical Mystique

OVERVIEW

Historically, the machine has been viewed both as evidence of the magnificent ingenuity of the human mind and as an example of the creature that destroys its creator. Scientists have been seen at various times as practitioners of magic, in league with the devil; as heretics, defying orthodox doctrine on how the world works; as arrogant intruders into the mysteries of nature, destroying the fragile balance of life. And they have also been acknowledged as stubborn seekers of reality and as benefactors of humanity.

Today the debate continues between those who see in the machine a hope for the worldwide improvement of the human lot and those who fear that, having become dependent upon the machine, people will be alienated from the human world. This polarity is fiercely present in esthetic, moral, and ecological issues.

To be able to make responsible decisions on those issues that radically affect our world and ourselves, we need a critical perspective; we need to know how machines in the past have both humanized and dehumanized society and how they continue to do both today. If we know what we want to make of our lives, we can more readily enjoy the benefits of the machine.

LEARNING OBJECTIVES

Having completed this module, you should be able to

1)   state various attitudes toward machines in different historical periods.

2)   state the ideas of individual artists and philosophers about the role of technology in human existence.

3)   indicate when and where the scientific method, as we now know it, began to emerge in human culture.

4)   compare contemporary distrust in the machine with ideas current in the Romantic era.

5)   point out significant events in the conflict between those who favored scientific progress and those who opposed it.

6)   respond to the criticism that the machine has made it unnecessary for people to do their own thinking.

7)　sum up the case for and against the machine as a boon to human existence. Suggestion: use television as a case in point.

8)　relate the film On the Bus to anti-technological thought.

AS YOU READ

Chapter 15: "The Mechanical Mystique"

1.　Be familiar with the theory concerning the abundance of slaves and the development of machines in the ancient world.

2.　In the Age of Pericles the Greeks expressed great faith in the human potential. How was this confidence reflected in their attitude toward machines? Contrast this view with that of the Romans.

3.　Be able to give examples of technology developed in medieval Europe in spite of--or because of--religious beliefs.

4.　How did the effects of the Bubonic plague in the fourteenth century lead eventually to progress in medical technology?

5.　Leonardo da Vinci epitomizes the Renaissance ideal of humanity. What apparently contradictory talents did he embody?

6.　In the Renaissance, concepts of power shifted from the power of God to the power of man. Show how this shift affected technological progress.

7.　Be able to explain the crisis in religious faith brought about by the discoveries of Copernicus and Galileo.

8.　In the Newtonian world view an analogy was made between the clock and the universe. Show how this analogy served to reconcile a mechanistic philosophy with Christian faith.

9.　Thomas Paine represented the religious, social, and political beliefs of many of his contemporary thinkers. Sum up these ideas.

10.　The poet William Blake spoke for those who saw the evils of industrialized society as the products of Isaac Newton's rational, scientific world view. What essential human quality did Blake believe that view denied?

11.　The Romantic era is characterized by certain prevailing beliefs about nature, the intellect and the emotions, human rights, and social class distinctions. Be able to identify expressions of these beliefs.

12.　Be able to explain how Mary Shelley's Frankenstein dramatizes typically Romantic ideas about the innocence and mystery of nature and the dehumanizing effects of scientific inquiry.

188

13. In what way can the concept of <u>luck</u> be considered a mechanical myth?

14. Give examples of music and the visual arts in which machines have played a significant part.

15. In response to the criticism that the machine relieves us of the need to think, cite evidence that our society is not indifferent to the active exercise of the mind.

VIEWING

I. <u>Television: The Electric Art</u>

--This program is about a specific medium of transmitting communication--television. The emphasis here is on what a mass medium does. That differences in perception exist when people experience reality at random is well known to the people responsible for TV shows. But since a mass medium is meant to have a mass influence, such randomness cannot be tolerated. Television has become almost an exact science. Millions are spent annually in researching its effects, especially how it can shape the buying habits of its audience.

--The comments made by Tay Voye indicate that "ratings" are the main source of research information. While networks cannot always predict what kind of show will be popular, you can be sure that ratings are profoundly analyzed each week by large staffs of experts, who try to determine what it is that appeals. The sponsors who pay the bills insist upon such analysis.

--The Ronny Zamora trial will be remembered longer than most murder trials if only for the unusual defense and some of the apparent facts that surfaced--for example, the average young person has viewed 18,000 murders on television by the time he has finished high school. While the jury remained unconvinced by the defense attorney's case and the testimony they heard, the full jury is still out when it comes to the influence of TV violence on a mass audience. How are murderers usually handled on TV? Are they glamorized in any way? Is it reasonable to think many people would (or do) try to imitate crimes they have seen? Does the medium itself make violence seem "less" violent somehow, less appalling?

--Ralph Renick, a newscaster, comments on the <u>selectivity</u> of television news coverage. "A gasoline tanker truck, overturned and on fire...makes a good picture." Nor must we forget that TV news programs are usually sponsored; hence they are as sensitive to ratings as entertainment shows.

--Vice President Spiro Agnew's somewhat historic denunciation of the news media may, in retrospect, appear more defensive and less aggressive than was originally thought. Nonetheless, Agnew did raise some points worth considering. <u>Do</u> the major newscasters have unlimited powers? <u>Do</u> they directly or indirectly influence the attitudes and voting habits of their huge audiences? Or, as others have suggested, are all of us victims of "communication overload" from the media, having turned numb and impervious to the messages assailing us day and night?

--Then there is that institution, the TV commercial. That such continual inter-ruptions to our sources of entertainment can affect our buying habits goes without saying; hence this program deals with another aspect: the commercial as art form. No doubt few take the trouble to notice the skill and imagination which often go into the conception and production of a 30 or 60 second communi-cation. After all, the situation and the characters must be almost instan-taneously established, then developed, then brought swiftly to a conclusion, leaving the viewer with a definite desire for the product or service. As you watch TV for pleasure, make note of some commercials that strike you as artistic --in the sense of carrying out their basic intentions cleverly. At any rate, looking for art is better than sitting there in disgust, isn't it? Besides, you don't have to be influenced.

II.   On the Bus

--The opening scenes contain real-life illustrations of dehumanized aspects of contemporary society. Among them you will see two works of sculpture by the artist Duane Hanson: Battlefield with Corpses and Motorcycle Wreck. These life-size fiberglass figures depict the shocking realities Hanson observed in our civilization during the 50s and 60s.

--People of the future are visualized as having none of the five senses. They lack any means of perceiving and responding to the world around them. These faceless characters are metaphors for people who have become so desensitized by the ugliness and violence of their environment they are incapable of human feeling. Note the irony in the statement that such a less-than-human condition could be a blessing.

--Observe that the features on some of the blank-faced people become visible and express feeling from time to time. Try to detect what kinds of experience restore, even momentarily, the human characteristics.

--A montage of scenes projects what the world might be like after the Final War of Human Beings. As you watch, try to identify the specific human needs that are not provided when civilization has been rebuilt.

--As you see the missiles and mushroom clouds of the Space War, you might wonder about the ultimate value of our technological skills if they are not controlled by the "human viewpoint."

--The final stage of dehumanization is made possible by eliminating parks, art galleries, theaters and then humanists themselves, from the design for a new society. Consider what threat humanistic values present to the survival of the kind of power called here "The Grand Council."

--At the end of the film, after the death of the last humanist, the young man refuses an invitation to ride on the bus. He says, "No thanks. I'd rather walk." Earlier in the film the narrator said about the city streets, "No one was just walking." If you consider the purpose and destination of the bus, the business of walking may take on a human significance. The young man's prefer-ence leaves us with two conflicting questions: will humanistic values ever be

190

completely eradicated, and can such one-person rebellions really accomplish anything?

--Since the bus is used in the program's title, there must be a very specific intent behind the phrase "on the bus." Or perhaps there are multiple meanings?

--A traditionally humanistic view of freedom pervades this program. While it may seem that the society as a whole has been enslaved by the Grand Council, the fact that all of the humanities have been banned--including the capacity for reflection--makes us wonder whether the Grand Council itself is not enslaved and the last humanist on earth is the only free person left. Certainly there is a parallel between his circumstances and those of Socrates, who, according to humanism, kept his freedom by giving up his life.

SELF-TEST

Match each item in the first column with an item in the second. Use no item more than one time.

T	1.	syllogism	anti-mechanistic theme	_____
V	2.	the Grand Council	impact of TV violence	_____
T	3.	Leonardo da Vinci	destruction of the naturally innocent by the arrogant intellect	_____
T	4.	William Paley	major influence on popular culture	_____
V	5.	Duane Hanson	there can be no clock without a clockmaker	_____
T	6.	Thomas Paine	new art form comparable to sonata	_____
T	7.	Isaac Newton	auto horns in orchestration	_____
V	8.	Brave New World	Common Sense	_____
T	9.	Frankenstein	saw the physical world as a perfectly functioning machine	_____
V	10.	Claes Oldenburg	can be offered as proof of superiority of the human mind	_____
VT	11.	mass media	machine-inspired visual artist	_____
T	12.	Shostakovich	denounced for dissonant and non-conformist music	_____
V	13.	Zamora trial	homo universale	_____
T	14.	TV commercials	executed the last humanist alive	_____
T	15.	George Gershwin	"Motorcycle Wreck"	_____

CHECK LIST OF MAIN IDEAS

1. Today as in past centuries relations between the humanists and the machine are uneasy.

2. Although some important later developments in science had their origins in the Middle Ages, Christian teaching, with its emphasis on salvation through penance and mortification of the flesh, would not have encouraged energy being spent on the development of labor-saving machines.

3. Respect for the machine increased in the Renaissance; the shift in emphasis on the significance of earthly life made it possible for people to see the machine as a product of human genius intended to render human life more pleasurable. The designs of Leonardo da Vinci foreshadowed many of our modern mechanical "miracles".

4. As civilization and science developed, plausible explanations were found for many previously unexplained phenomena, yet many questions remain unanswered.

5. The human misery and the devastation of natural resources resulting from the industrialization of cities focused the wrath of the Romantics on technological progress.

6. Though the pendulum of thought has swung to the side of science there is evidence that many people are seeking alternatives NOT provided by laboratories or computers.

7. It is well to keep a humanistic perspective, to insist on freedom to choose how best to use machines to promote a fully human existence.

RECOMMENDED READING

Fernand Braudel, The Structures of Everyday Life, vol. I of Civilization and
    Capitalism 15th-18th Century (New York: Harper & Row, 1981). This is a work in
    progress, which, when completed, will offer a definitive study of the inner
    workings of capitalism from its roots in the twilight of the Middle Ages. Of
    particular interest to our study in the present chapter is the author's in-depth
    knowledge of technological advances and the reasons for them.

James Burke, The Day the Universe Changed (Boston: Little Brown, 1984). The
    author's underlying thesis is that the universe has "changed" at milestone
    points whenever a new way of looking at it came along. The opening sentence
    tells a great deal: "You are what you know." By this he means, of course, that
    one is trapped within the historical context in which one happens to be born.
    Everything one thinks one knows is controlled by the cosmic view of the times.
    Of value is the insight given to us concerning the way science looks at our
    world today.

Arthur C. Clarke, 2001: A Space Odyssey (New York: New American Library, 1968).
    The novel was based on the screenplay of the now classic film written by Clarke
    and director Stanley Kubrick, but in the opinion of a growing number of discern-
    ing readers, a significant work on its own merit. The entire work can be read
    in one sitting, and every reader is recommended to do just that. Particularly
    intense is the literary account of the developing relationship between astronaut
    Dave Bowman and Hal, the computer, who (which?) is a unique antagonistic force,
    since it (he?) is not exactly evil, but nonetheless chilling in its mechanical
    perfection.

Mary Shelley, Frankenstein, or The Modern Prometheus (Berkeley: University of
    California Press, 1984). Recently republished, and with stunning illustrations
    by Barry Moser, this neglected literary milestone seems ready for a genuine
    revival, especially in view of its astonishing anticipation of today's anti-
    nuclear protests.

Alvin Toffler, Future Shock (See Recommended Reading, Module XI.)

Barbara Tuchman, A Distant Mirror (New York: Alfred A. Knopf, 1978). Probably no
    work has ever offered as much insight into the 14th century as this study by an
    historian who writes like a novelist. Of particular interest to readers of the
    present book is the material on the Great Plague and its profound effect on the
    destiny of the human race, an effect we are still feeling.

Survey 7

1. Nietzsche originally used Apollo and Dionysus as psychological labels in his analysis of responses to tragedy. In his opinion, which of the following represented an UNDESIRABLE response?

   1. strong emotionalism
   2. looking mainly for moral instruction
   3. an unthinking involvement in the passions of the drama
   4. being less immediately concerned with the play's message
   5. 1, 3, and 4 are correct.

2. All of the following characteristics are representative of the Apollonian state of mind EXCEPT

   1. clarity.
   2. spontaneity.
   3. order.
   4. reason.
   5. control.

3. One of the following was cited in the TV program The Sunlit Chariot as an example of the tragic consequences of an Apollonian social order. It was

   1. New England Puritanism.
   2. the Sacco-Vanzetti case.
   3. Einstein's equation for the conversion of mass and energy.
   4. the Mardi Gras in New Orleans.
   5. the violent death of children in Lord of the Flies.

4. If you were invited to a Dionysian banquet, you would be MOST likely to discover which of the following?

   1. an abundance of food
   2. rare and exotic herbs
   3. vegetarian dishes
   4. a well-balanced yin and yang diet
   5. sensuous musical accompaniment for each course

5. The dreams which come to our unconscious in sleep are Dionysian because

195

1. they are beyond our control.
2. we can analyze them and increase our self-knowledge.
3. they symbolize stages in the life cycle.
4. they represent acknowledged self-punishment for past misdeeds.
5. they represent the reestablishment of an inner order.

6. The fact that the central character of On the Bus is willing to feel and show emotion is suggested by

   1. the passionate speech he makes to the Grand Council.
   2. the letters he writes to the woman who once loved him.
   3. the fact that the woman who once loved him loses her face when in his presence.
   4. the fact that he has never lost his face.
   5. the fact that the young student remembers him, even though the student has become a member of the Secret Police.

7. Apollo is to Dionysus as

   1. spring is to winter.
   2. the Boston Tea Party was to King George.
   3. atomic energy is to atomic structure.
   4. the moon launch is to moonlight.
   5. intuition is to inspiration.

8. The Dionysian spirit is applicable to which of the following artistic creations?

   1. the formal gardens at Versailles
   2. the structural design of St. Peter's in Rome
   3. the balanced composition of a landscape painting
   4. the improvised musical excursions of a jazz performer
   5. the geometric principle which holds the Gothic cathedral in place

9. In the conflict between Apollo and Dionysus as social forces, history tends to show that

   1. the Apollonian inevitably wins out.
   2. the Dionysian is eventually overcome.
   3. there is always a balance between Apollo and Dionysus.
   4. each force tends to generate its own opposite.
   5. both 1 and 2 are correct.

10. Apollo and Dionysus are symbols of often conflicting extremes in the world of education. Which of the following observations best describes the Apollo/ Dionysus relationship in education?

    1. Education which stresses rote learning is predominantly Dionysian.
    2. Innovative classrooms, stressing student creativity, are Apollonian in nature.
    3. The emphasis on creative responses in education is primarily Dionysian.
    4. An over-abundance of administrators in a school is a Dionysian factor.
    5. Apollonian instructors probably give fewer exams than their Dionysian counterparts.

11. Which of the following **best** reflects an Apollonian viewpoint?

     1. We should follow the emotional thrust of human existence.
     2. Humans should reject reason in life in order to realize the self through intuition.
     3. The only reliable guides for living are instinct and feelings.
     4. The universe can be understood by the rational mind.
     5. The pleasures of youth are all the more precious for their brevity.

12. Which of the following Apollo/Dionysus relationships would probably produce the most advanced and the happiest society?

     1. Dionysus in the governor's chair; Apollo in the arts
     2. a succession of Apollonian rulers
     3. a free and easy Dionysian spirit in government, education, and art
     4. an Apollonian discipline in government, education, and art
     5. none of the above

13. Which of the following statements can be used to explain what McLuhan means by "The medium is the message?"

     1. A TV commercial does not say what a magazine ad says.
     2. You cannot really translate what a piece of music is saying into the language of sculpture.
     3. Look around a shopping center, and you will discover many assumptions about the customers and their way of life.
     4. A novel cannot actually be made into a movie.
     5. Any of the above.

14. The program Dionysus: Ecstasy and Renewal dealt with a number of manifestations of the Dionysian spirit, including carnivals. According to the film, "carnival" was originally a medieval festival, and the term meant

     1. obscene frolic.
     2. weekend madness.
     3. farewell to the flesh.
     4. let loose the dogs.
     5. fun and games.

15. One of the video programs is titled The Sunlit Chariot. The meaning of this title is made quite clear early in the film. To what does the title refer?

     1. the classical monarchy of the ancient world
     2. the vehicle Apollo drove across the sky
     3. the wild excesses of Dionysus which nonetheless created civilization
     4. the bus which took joyous young people through Europe
     5. the revolutionary zeal of the French peasantry

16. Dionysus: Ecstasy and Renewal begins with a beach scene in which a group of boys construct and then destroy an elaborate sand castle. What does this act symbolize in the program?

     1. the romantic view of children

2. impressionistic interpretation of the adult world
3. the cycle of order and chaos
4. the human quest for perfect form
5. the adult world in which problems are solved rationally

17. The textbook alludes to Art Deco-inspired machine designs as evidence that

1. humanists continue to view the machine with distrust.
2. the machine continues to be as esthetically exciting as ever to visual artists.
3. the style of Art Deco indicates an indifference to artistic taste as a result of the Great Depression.
4. twentieth century art is inferior to nineteenth century art when it deals with the artist's alienation from nature.
5. the artist sees the machine-orientation of Art Deco as a source of financial reward in a world where artists are seldom affluent.

18. In the society depicted in On the Bus, which human trait is NOT tolerated?

1. industry
2. conformity
3. curiosity
4. mindlessness
5. apathy

19. In the discussion of mechanical tendencies in our present-day attitudes, the most mechanical of our myths is identified as our faith in

1. computers.
2. X-rays.
3. lasers.
4. progress.
5. luck.

20. According to The Electric Art, the fact that Ronny Zamora was found guilty of murder indicates that, in at least some minds,

1. teenagers watch television too much.
2. television cannot be held directly responsible for a person's actions.
3. the television medium is its message.
4. television newscasters have the power to distort the truth.
5. the television medium was itself on trial.

21. According to the program Television: The Electric Art, a television commercial can sometimes be evaluated as one would evaluate which of the following literary forms:

1. sonnet
2. short story
3. novel
4. a Shakespearean play
5. chamber theater

22. <u>The Sunlit Chariot</u> contained a long segment about Einstein's effort to prevent the dropping of the first atomic bomb. What was Einstein's apparent motive?

    1. He was not being given the proper recognition for his role in creating the bomb.
    2. He had a deep-rooted interest in the traditions and culture of the East.
    3. He had no idea that the project on which he was working would produce an atom bomb.
    4. He was fearful of the uncontrolled uses of atomic energy.
    5. He found himself pressured by many pacifist groups he did not wish to antagonize.

23. In ancient Greek myths the attitude toward machines was generally that

    1. they were evidence of human greatness.
    2. they belonged in the realm of the gods.
    3. they were necessary evils for the relief of human drudgery.
    4. they would one day assist mankind in its strife against the gods.
    5. they were beneficial in the pursuit of knowledge about the world of nature.

24. The point is made that technology advances in a society when

    1. there are more slaves than masters.
    2. labor is scarce.
    3. people have leisure to invent.
    4. a laissez faire system of economics prevails.
    5. there is a long period of peace between wars.

25. All but one of the following are reasons why technology developed very slowly in the Middle Ages. Which is not given as a reason?

    1. The Christian church emphasized salvation rather than comfort and ease.
    2. People were generally well off in a state of nature without the need for technology.
    3. The church taught that everything happens according to God's will; hence there is no point in humans striving to improve their material lot.
    4. Since human beings are by their very nature imperfect, so are their works.
    5. The church prohibited studies such as medicine that required technical knowledge.

26. Which one of the following statements can <u>not</u> be accurately made about Leonardo da Vinci's scientific investigations:

    1. He was scientifically interested in the circulation of the blood.
    2. He was proficient in aerodynamics.
    3. He produced the first computer.
    4. He was a meteorologist.
    5. He invented the hydrometer.

27. An underlying theme of Chapter 15 is that

    1. there is clear danger that machines will end up dehumanizing the people in our society.

2. it is possible for human beings to interact creatively with machines.
3. machines alienate us from the natural world.
4. life in a state of nature is preferable to life in a technological society.
5. even slavery is preferable to a machine-dominated society.

28. A culture that had a strong impact on interest in science in the Renaissance was

   1. French.
   2. Italian.
   3. Islamic.
   4. Indian.
   5. British.

29. Deism postulated that

   1. creation was the Divine act of bestowing order on pre-existing matter that was in a state of chaos.
   2. God created a world perfectly governed by natural laws and then withdrew, leaving it to run itself.
   3. the universe is mysterious, ultimately not intelligible to the human mind.
   4. God intervenes in the affairs of the world to mete out rewards for virtue and punishment for wickedness.
   5. the perfect functioning of the physical universe is evidence that it was not the produce of a divine creator but the result of purely natural phenomena.

30. An analogy that helped reconcile religion with science in the eighteenth century was that of the universe and

   1. the rose.
   2. the waterwheel.
   3. the clock.
   4. the circle.
   5. the life of a human being.

31. For Thomas Paine proof of the existence of God lay in

   1. the scriptures.
   2. the evidence of order in the physical world.
   3. a mystical apprehension going beyond rational thought.
   4. an analogy with an orderly government.
   5. the authority of theologians.

32. The Declaration of Independence and the Constitution were largely the product of the thinking of what group?

   1. Scholastic metaphysicians
   2. Lutherans
   3. Tories
   4. Industrialists
   5. Deists

33. The plot of Mary Shelley's Frankenstein revolves around the theme, popular in the Romantic period, that

1. the simple life is nobler than the one lived in luxury.
2. in the natural state all people are equal.
3. capitalism exploits the masses of humble people.
4. human beings are destructive when they pry into the secrets of nature.
5. a democratic state holds more potential for human rights than a monarchy does.

34. The discussion of Zen and the Art of Motorcycle Maintenance brings out the idea that

1. motorcycles pollute the air more than do automobiles with emission control systems.
2. it is possible to use the machine as a way to live with more conscious awareness of one's environment.
3. motorcycles are more energy efficient than automobiles.
4. since you can't trust professional mechanics, you should learn to maintain your own machines.
5. bikers' lifestyles are anti-humanist.

MODULE XV

Themes in the Humanities: Freedom

OVERVIEW

Like love and happiness, two themes already explored in this course, freedom is something everybody talks about, and indeed something for which many continue to die. Yet it too is capable of many definitions, depending upon time, circumstances, and one's philosophy of life.

B. F. Skinner and the behaviorists tell us that no one, in fact, exists in a state that can meaningfully be called free--that people are the sum total of forces operating on them. The logical thing, some behaviorists believe, is to create a science of behavioral engineering that will condition people to be peaceful, hardworking, and law-abiding.

A characteristic position taken by humanists, however, is that people _can_ be free to make meaningful choices among significant alternatives, provided that they take responsibility for their actions. In this module we consider arguments both for and against the existence of freedom.

LEARNING OBJECTIVES

Having completed this module, you should be able to

1) identify possible support for the view that there is free will.

2) identify the support for determinism which has been provided by behavioral schools in biology and psychology.

3) identify other arguments against freedom of the will.

4) describe some elements in what B. F. Skinner calls a "technology of behavior."

5) identify objections to behaviorism which are sometimes raised by humanists.

6) single out viewpoints in the free will/determinism controversy which appear personally relevant.

7) state some reasons that John Webster's _Duchess of Malfi_ is relevant to considerations of freedom.

8) relate the character of Huckleberry Finn to Rousseau's theory of the origin and nature of social institutions.

9) relate Rousseau's <u>Man With the Stick</u> to the problem of freedom.

AS YOU READ

Chapter 16: "Freedom"

1. Many cite the Bill of Rights without knowing precisely what it involves. Do you?

2. Those who believe that human beings are by nature either exploiters or the exploited often overlook the fact that sometimes the exploited freely choose their role rather than assume the responsibilities accruing to exploiters. If a choice exists, then how is either role "basic" to human nature?

3. Rousseau believed that not the Man with the Stick (the exploiter) but the social institutions were responsible for the evils in society. But lacking any controls, what would people do with the Man with the Stick? Rosseau urged that he be dealt with directly by the people--that is, through revolution. Does revolution in this sense cure the evils in society?

4. Nietzsche said some people like to be masters and others like to be slaves. Was he right? Or do the slaves (the exploited) always have a reason for their plight other than choice? Do you think the conditions of their plight affect the choices they make?

5. What is Hegel's theory of the dialectic? How can it be used to interpret the Apollonian/Dionysian conflict?

6. How did Marx apply Hegel's theory in his interpretation of how economic power could be balanced?

7. How have present day socialist countries (e.g., USSR and China) departed from Marx's dictums? Do they represent a synthesis of conflicting views?

8. Granted that a governmental bureaucracy exists in any society which calls itself free, are its citizens exploited? Or can they be said to have alternatives to exploitation?

9. Is it better to have a consistent, predictable character--thus to be unable to face unlimited choices--or to be able always to act in an unpredictable inconsistent manner?

10. Has the recent sexual revolution made Freud's theories obsolete? Or do you believe society still tends to be mainly Victorian in its attitudes toward sex?

11. Many persons, including humanists, would object to the interpretation that humans harbor an unconscious desire to return to the womb. Why do you think it is important for people to think their actions are not determined by conditions which took place during their infantile stages?

12. Skinner's view is that human nature has an innate capacity to be conditioned, that humanity is never free. Skinner uses a "technology of behavior" as the method of reaching an ideal society. Would a humanist agree with Skinner's ultimate goal? With his methodology? With the assumption that such a goal is feasible?

13. What do sociobiologists mean when they say that human behavior can be interpreted in terms of genetic self-interest? Can you think of a concrete example of human behavior that cannot be accounted for by this new science?

14. Could Skinner argue against Schopenhauer's belief that it is impossible for a person to have a direct experience of his will?

15. Genetics, the science of heredity, has not yet become a branch of philosophy, but it has become so pervasive in our culture that arguments about free will almost certainly have to take it into account. The day may not be far off when large numbers of people will trace their physical characteristics and their intelligence to genetic engineering practices, and the question will be: Can any argument be advanced to support the idea that their will is in any way free?

16. Be able to sum up William James's argument against pure determinism.

VIEWING

I. A Cry of Freedom

--What is freedom? What do we mean when we use the term? Can if be defined? Many definitions exist, from many sources--suggesting that a desire for something people call freedom may be well-nigh universal in human societies, though no universal agreement exists as to what the concept "freedom" is.

--The Greeks and Romans talked of freedom of thought and action. Socrates believed that man's unique attribute was his capacity for rational thought and that therefore man must be endowed with the freedom to exercise it. Freedom meant the liberation of the good man from bad attitudes and hence bad actions. "Socrates's message for the ages is that freedom is moral integrity, and has nothing to do with the restrictions, the death, imposed upon one by society... and moral dishonesty is enslavement, no matter how much privilege one may appear to enjoy."

--Christianity, mainly through the work of St. Augustine, confronted the question of man's freedom in a world created by an omnipotent deity, one with foreknowledge of what his creatures would do. Augustine argued that because Adam, having had the freedom to choose good or evil, chose evil, he had to bear the consequences of his act; one of these consequences was a continuation of the need to choose between the two. This choice constituted the moral drama of man's existence--and its meaning. Later on, an authoritarian church provided codes that one had to accept and to obey if one were to be saved. Salvation, not freedom, became the first priority of the medieval mind.

205

--Roger Bacon, a 13th century English monk, often considered the father of the scientific method, seemed to view freedom as liberation from superstition and fear . . . even as Socrates had viewed it as the liberation of the good man from bad attitudes. Thus the question may be raised: is the history of freedom really the history of "liberation movements"? If people are not fighting for a specific set of rights, are they actively, _meaningfully_ free?

--The 18th century philosopher Jean-Jacques Rousseau advanced the theory that man is born free but becomes shackled by the institutions of society. He looked back to a golden age before civilization, when mankind lived in harmony with nature. He hypothesized a creature he called the Noble Savage who possessed all the natural virtues civilized man had lost. Therefore, he argued for a return to nature when these gifts could be reclaimed and man could rediscover his natural integrity. It was an alluring dream, but it offered simplistic answers in an irreversibly complex world. Nonetheless, we still hear voices crying out for a return to the "natural."

--Mark Twain replayed Rousseau's theme in his masterpiece The Adventures of Huckleberry Finn (1884). Huck, the "uncivilizable" free spirit, becomes his author's critical spokesman, questioning the institutions of American society and rejecting its repressive powers. But the reader, fantasize as he might about living Huck's unencumbered existence, might come away with serious reservations. To whom or what is Huck responsible, except his own good sense and his fierce will? Would a million Hucks create a fine and noble society--or a chaotic one?

--Perhaps in the final analysis freedom is an idea, an ideal--"an indefinable inward feeling, a mysterious insight achieved only by the rare few who brave the struggle--heroes like Socrates, Buddha, Mahatma Gandhi, Martin Luther King. . ." These were people who made noble choices, stood behind their actions, and paid a heavy price.

II.   The World Was All Before Them

--This final program in the course is, as you can see, a series of excerpts from all of the other programs but arranged in such a way as to suggest the humanist's vision of life.

--The identity of the narrator is most mysterious. There are a number of possibilities, but viewers should have the fun of deciding for themselves.

--The narration requires careful listening. The meaning of the program lies in its structure, as the narrator goes from an extremely bleak and pessimistic view of humanity to a conclusion that is not so bleak. Try to define this conclusion. Try to determine what led the narrator to it. Where do you stand on the matter?

--The title of this film is taken from John Milton's poem, Paradise Lost, the great epic account of Adam and Eve's fall from innocence in the Garden of Eden. As the poem ends, Adam and Eve begin the exile which is a consequence of the Fall. The point here is that, even though Adam and Eve are being punished for their sin, paradoxically they now know that the essence of being human is to have freedom of choice:

206

The world was all before them, where to choose
Their place of rest, and Providence their guide.
They, hand in hand, with wandering steps and slow,
Through Eden took their solitary way.

SELF-TEST

Match each item in the first column with an item in the second. Use no item more than one time.

T 1. <u>Man with the Stick</u>   scientific method can liberate _____
                                          people from superstition

T 2. People are either   genetic investment   _____
       masters or slaves
                                          determinism   _____
T 3. economic version of
       thesis/antithesis/synthesis   freedom is moral integrity   _____

T 4. character consistency   satirizes repressiveness   _____
                                          of American society

T 5. sociobiology
                                          Nietzsche   _____
T 6. only the insane are always
       and completely free   argument against freedom   _____
                                          of the will
T 7. freedom defined as effort
       to escape from unpleasant   Skinner   _____
       consequences
                                          hypothesized the Noble Savage   _____
T 8. that we can regret past
       actions proves freedom   Marx   _____
       is possible
                                          indeterminism   _____
T 9. psychological determinism
                                          myth figure responsible   _____
V 10. Rousseau   for origins of civil society

V 11. Socrates   Freud

V 12. <u>Huckleberry Finn</u>

V 13. Roger Bacon

207

CHECK LIST OF MAIN IDEAS

1. The humanist approach to life is based upon the freedom to make rational choices among significant alternatives.

2. Controversy exists over whether human beings are free agents. The major conflicting positions are:

    determinism: man's life and his actions are predetermined or conditioned--he has no free will.

    Freudian psychology: the environment shapes man's psyche and greatly influences his behavior.

    sociobiology: a new form of determinism which holds that behavior is governed biologically, to ensure survival of the individual's genes.

    indeterminism: since at times we regret past choices, free will is a real possibility.

    libertarianism: everyone can be free; no one needs to be bound by his character, the unconscious mind, or any other external force.

3. A major spokesman for determinism is B. F. Skinner, a behavioral psychologist, who argues that humanists mistakenly believe human dignity depends upon establishing a case for freedom. For Skinner, freedom is liberation from something unpleasant.

4. In the individual, freedom can be achieved by willingness to break old patterns and explore new pathways, and by self-imposed limitations, substituting internal for external reinforcements.

FREEDOM AND HUMANISM

by

Donald M. Early

The conviction persists that freedom and humanity are somehow inseparably linked, and that we cannot hope to understand ourselves until we have some understanding of their relationship. We ask "Am I free to direct my life, make choices that are genuinely mine, make moral decisions that affect not only me and those about me, but possibly the larger cosmos as well? Or am I without any true volition, simply the tool of destiny . . . perhaps no more than a creature of blind chance?"

Any assumptions we make in these matters--and they can only be assumptions--are of prime importance, for ultimately they affect what meaning, if any, we discover in human life, and in our separate existence.

If we take the position of the determinist, we will say that individuals are not free in any way, that the whole enterprise (of which each is the minutest part) is out of their hands. The universe is a system of inflexible laws, and every particle of matter, every spark of life, every thought, every act is nothing but a reflex of those laws. Whatever influence people think they have over events is purely illusory--as if a wave were to think it had stirred the ocean into a storm.

Such concepts have their roots in 19th century scientific belief, which in turn affected other areas of thought: philosophy, sociology, anthropology, art, and even religion. Determinism is still a valid position for some philosophers, who doubtless find in it the satisfaction of knowing beyond any doubt that the universe is wholly without meaning in any humanistic sense.

If, on the other hand, we take the existentialist's view, we will say that humankind, cast adrift on a sea of nothing, and inescapably alone, suffers a terrible freedom--a freedom in which each individual's survival depends upon the ability to "create" self, one's own reality of being. No purpose can be attached to the universe except what one painfully fabricates from fragments of experience that in themselves have no meaning. Humankind is absolutely alone--hence, absolutely free.

The world, in the existentialist's view, is a kind of fortuitous dream, or rather nightmare, beset with all the terrors of undifferentiated possibility. Existentialism is unquestionably the headiest brew modern philosophy has yet concocted, though for some it lacks any soothing, any comforting ingredients. To say "man is condemned to freedom" is to say that he is forced into the terror of choosing, and perhaps choosing wrong.

The determinist and the existentialist occupy extreme positions in philosophy. Most humanist thinkers, on the other hand, tend to avoid the extremes--certainly in areas as clouded with ambiguity as the subject of freedom is--and to assume that in a field of contending forces or opposing views, the truth, or what can be allowed to serve as truth, stands somewhere near the middle. They see a kind of triadic process at work here: from two opposite, interacting elements, a third, synthetic element is born that represents superior insight.

Modern science, which has provided many new insights into humanity's physical and psychological nature, and into its evolutionary history as well, has also provided bases for new speculations on the problem of human freedom. Among such speculations is the idea that freedom may not be something that humanity either has or does not have, but rather something that it may have the capacity to create. Freedom is seen not as a gift (or a gift withheld), but as potentiality implicit in the evolutionary venture. Freedom is something to be earned.

It is quite possible that for most of its history humanity has not been free in any positive sense of the word. Human actions and thought may simply have followed guidelines inherent in the human condition, the result of a limited power over the environment and the sequence of events. According to one modern savant (Julian Jaynes, The Origins of Consciousness in the Breakdown of the Bicameral Mind) mankind before about 3,000 B. C. was not conscious at all in the present sense of the word. Before then, Jaynes tells us, people got their signals from inner voices which they called gods. The inner voices came from the right hemisphere of the brain; the left hemisphere constituted the "human" side of the brain. This meant that ancient people lived psychologically in a bicameral world--that is, their governing faculties consisted of two relatively separate powers. Only the eventual breakdown of this arrangement--and the accompanying decay of the gods--made it possible for people to become conscious in our modern sense--to become self-conscious, self-aware, self-analytical. With consciousness, people gained the ability to deliberate, to pause between stimulus and response, to decide. No longer bound to obey external authority, they now found authority and understanding within their newly conscious self. In short, they began to be free.

Such a radical hypothesis, of course, awaits proof. Its value here is as a dramatic indicator of the direction modern thought may be moving toward: a concept of freedom as process, a thing to be achieved when people have reached the stage where they can "deserve" it.

It can be argued that we are at that stage now. For have not the enormous powers conferred by science given us enormous freedom to use or misuse them? Through technology, we now have the power to reshape the environment along artificial, and therefore uniquely human, ways; we find ourselves deciding which species on earth we will or will not preserve; we consider how the atmosphere may be altered, how climate and weather may eventually be controlled. Already we envision our ability, through genetic management, to blueprint our biological future; cloning is only one of the more spectacular possibilities hinted at. Most significantly of all, we possess the terrible freedom utterly to annihilate the world in an atomic holocaust

Of course, there are those who argue that all these "supposed" freedoms are but stages in a predestined plan to have humanity self-destruct at a certain point. Technology is seen as merely the means of carrying out that end.

210

Such thinking, however, will strike most of us as the counsel of despair. IF humanity can get past the technological crisis, IF we can avoid annihilating ourselves as well as the planet, then the possibility of almost unlimited freedom emerges: freedom to develop our intelligence by learning to use the now-unused three-quarters of the brain, to achieve new levels of spirit and creativity, to make ourselves what we have always boasted we were--the center of our universe--and perhaps the inseminator of other universes undreamed of, light years away.

RECOMMENDED READING

Norman O. Brown. Life Against Death (Middleton, Conn.: Wesleyan University Press, 1959). For the ambitious reader, a brilliant if cynical interpretation of history in terms of Freud's contentions that human civilization is rooted in neuroses and human "progress" is a long march toward self-destruction.

Aldous Huxley. Brave New World (See Recommended Reading, Module V.)

William James, "The Dilemma of Determinism" in The Will to Believe and Other Essays in Popular Philosophy (See Recommended Reading, Module V.) This short and precisely written essay written essay takes the determinist position and turns it back, knife-like, on its supporters. By pushing the position to its logical extreme, James paints a grim picture of a universe which wills that disasters occur; for chance accidents can happen only in an undetermined world.

Karl Marx and Friedrich Engels. Basic Writings on Politics and Philosophy ed. Lewis S. Fever (Garden City, N. Y.: Doubleday & Co., 1959). A fine selection of the major Marxist statements, including the 1848 Communist Manifesto. There is an excellent introduction which does considerable summarizing.

B. F. Skinner. Beyond Freedom and Dignity (New York: Alfred A. Knopt, 1971). This book by the author of Walden II (Module XIII) argues that the resistance to behavioral theory in the name of human freedom and dignity fails to understand that these terms have no meaning as pure ideals. Both are brought about by conditioning factors.

John Webster. The Duchess of Malfi (Appears in various editions). Possibly the most distinguished work of the Elizabethan theater not by Shakespeare, this is a powerful tragedy about human greed, jealousy, and enslavement to power--and the fact that even the righteous inevitably suffer.

Edward Wilson. Sociobiology: The New Synthesis (Cambridge, Mass.: Harvard University Press, 1975). In this definitive work, the author sets forth the general biological principles that govern social behavior and organization in all kinds of animals, including humans.

1. The narrator of the final program <u>The World Was All Before Them</u> is evidently some conscious power observing the Earth from some external vantage point. What conclusion does he reach about the inhabitants of Earth?

   1. They will end up destroying themselves.
   2. Too often they lose hope without realizing that things always work out for the best.
   3. They keep making mistakes, but somehow they keep opening up new possibilities for themselves.
   4. Despite their pretensions to civilization, human beings are basically animals.
   5. Earthlings are at a very primitive level of development compared to beings on distant planets.

2. Humanists often are appalled by Skinner's proposed technology of behavior, prophesying a sterile future society without creativity or excitement. Skinner bases his proposal on which of the following contentions?

   1. The masses are incapable of thinking for themselves.
   2. Creativity can be sacrificed in the interest of social order.
   3. Since none escapes conditioning, why not condition intelligently?
   4. Contrary to humanistic belief, science is a highly creative field.
   5. If behaviorists do not design society's future, tyrants will.

3. Which of the following areas of inquiry does not support determinism?

   1. Schopenhauer's theory of will
   2. Freud's theory of the mind
   3. Skinner's theory of conditioning
   4. sociobiology
   5. Newton's world picture

4. Nietzsche's <u>Übermensch</u> has been viewed in both a positive and negative light. One can, however, make a neutral statement about him that neither supports nor rejects the concept. It is that the <u>Übermensch</u>

   1. persuades others to accept his vision of reality.

2. is, after all, only following God's orders.
3. is capable of altruism without having to surrender much self-interest.
4. seeks to attract fanatic cults in order to maintain his power.
5. is entitled to exploit those with a slave mentality.

5. A major humanistic objection to behavioral thinking can be expressed in which of the following ways?

1. Negative reinforcement is demeaning to human dignity.
2. Psychoanalysts are overly preoccupied with sexual causes.
3. History does not reduce itself to economic cycles.
4. Nothing requires a conditioning force to be external to the individual.
5. Behavioral engineering is cruel and inhuman.

6. Which of the following headlines would appear to support or conflict with your own views on the matter of determinism versus free will?

1. PRESIDENT SIGNS UP FOR MAIDEN SPACE FLIGHT, CLAIMING HE IS IN HANDS OF PROVIDENCE
2. CASTRO SEES FALL OF OIL CARTELS AS INEVITABLE
3. LET STATE ASSUME CARE OF GIFTED CHILDREN, PROGRESSIVE PARTY URGES
4. "I WANT TO PAY MY DEBT TO SOCIETY" CRIES CONVICTED MURDER
5. "LEGALIZE COCAINE!" CRIES BEST-SELLING AUTHOR OF DO YOUR THING

7. The libertarian position receives support from all of the following except ONE. Which is it?

1. Newton's world picture
2. the philosophy of indeterminism
3. Schopenhauer's theory of will
4. a sense of regret over past mistakes
5. Saint Augustine's view of freedom

8. One of the following philosophers maintained that all of nature was an objectification of the will. His name was

1. Marx.
2. Skinner.
3. Baron d'Holbach.
4. Schopenhauer.
5. General William S. Booth.

9. The program A Cry of Freedom suggests that in the final analysis such people as Socrates, Gandhi, and King may be among the rare few in history who can be considered truly free. What did they have in common that made them free?

1. Their actions were always unpredictable.
2. They managed to keep from being imprisoned.
3. They led armed revolts against authoritarianism.
4. They knew they had a price to pay, and paid it.
5. Each won a long court battle in which he sued the state for an invasion of privacy.

10. Which statement best expresses the main idea behind the film A Cry of Freedom?

1. Humanity has always experienced a burning desire to be free.
2. People would rather follow than lead.
3. To be free, one must accept and deal with some limitations.
4. After a revolution there is usually chaos in society.
5. Revolution has historically proved to be the most successful means of liberating the oppressed.

11. The program A Cry of Freedom offered an historical perspective on the concept of freedom, pointing out that, while Socrates may have personified the ideal of freedom, the concept itself was not part of Greek thought. Which of the following is the first thinker positively to address the subject of freedom directly?

    1. Nathan Hale
    2. George Washington
    3. St. Augustine
    4. Julius Ceaser
    5. Mark Twain

12. One of the video programs singles out Huck Finn as a very significant American hero. What MAJOR reason is given for Huck's stature in our literature?

    1. He exemplifies American grit and its triumph over foreign dandyism.
    2. He is free of any racist or sexist attitudes.
    3. He represents the inevitable conquest of the wilderness by the advancing forces of civilization.
    4. He is the poor citizen forced to conform to and obey the oppressive laws of society.
    5. He is a Dionysian spirit needed to counteract an Apollonian society.

13. The World Was All Before Them takes both its title and its final viewpoint about humanity from an epic poem about Adam and Eve and the loss of Eden. This poem was written by

    1. John Milton.
    2. William Shakespeare.
    3. Elizabeth Barrett Browning.
    4. John Donne.
    5. Walt Whitman.

14. Altering the nature of the molecule in order to bring about a prearranged result belongs to

    1. the philosophy of indeterminism.
    2. the science of geophysics.
    3. Schopenhauer's analysis of the will objectified.
    4. the practice of genetic engineering.
    5. the imposition of limits on the self so as to free the will.

15. A Cry of Freedom begins and ends with a young man's leaving home. Which of the following best describes his mood as the program ends?

    1. Freedom does not exist.

214

2. It is better to be disciplined than to be free.
3. Marx was right: money is what we're really after.
4. Now that I'm supposedly free, what do I do?
5. There must be more to life than floating on a raft.

16. Which of the following is NOT an element of Hegel's dialectic method of thinking?

   1. synthesis
   2. symbiosis
   3. thesis
   4. antithesis
   5. analysis

ANSWERS TO SELF-TESTS

Module I: 8, 7, 1, 9, 6, 12, 10, 11, 4, 3, 5, 2

Module II: 4, 16, 9, 11, 10, 15, 2, 1, 17, 5, 3, 6, 14, 18, 8, 13, 12, 7

Module III: 10, 14, 5, 11, 9, 2, 4, 13, 3, 7, 8, 1, 6, 12

Module IV A: 2, 5, 11, 6, 12, 9, 1, 10, 8, 4, 3, 7, 13

         B: 6, 8, 3, 5, 9, 7, 2, 4, 10, 1

Module V: 12, 7, 8, 11, 1, 13, 10, 9, 3, 2, 6, 4, 5

Module VI: 14, 9, 1, 12, 6, 3, 15, 2, 13, 8, 5, 11, 7, 10, 4

Module VII: 11, 4, 5, 6, 7, 12, 3, 2, 1, 9, 10, 8

Module VIII A: 7, 10, 3, 5, 1, 4, 2, 6, 9, 8

         B: 8, 6, 1, 7, 4, 9, 2, 10, 5, 3

Module IX: 11, 3, 9, 4, 6, 8, 1, 5, 7, 2, 10

Module X: 2, 9, 10, 4, 8, 1, 7, 13, 12, 5, 3, 11, 14, 6

Module XI: 10, 13, 1, 4, 9, 3, 12, 2, 6, 7, 8, 11, 5

Module XII: 5, 14, 8, 4, 9, 13, 1, 10, 3, 6, 12, 7, 2, 11

Module XIII: 3, 7, 8, 11, 9, 12, 10, 13, 5, 1, 2, 14, 4, 15, 6

Module XIV: 8, 13, 9, 11, 4, 14, 15, 6, 7, 1, 10, 12, 3, 2, 5

Module XV: 13, 5, 6, 11, 12, 2, 4, 7, 10, 3, 8, 1, 9